The Rejuvenation Strategy

The Rejuvenation Strategy

A Medically Approved
Fitness Program
to Reverse the Effects
of Aging

RENÉ CAILLIET, M.D.,
AND LEONARD GROSS

DOUBLEDAY & COMPANY, INC.
GARDEN CITY, NEW YORK
1987

Library of Congress Cataloging-in-Publication Data
Cailliet, René.
Rejuvenation Strategy, The
1. Physical fitness.   2. Exercise.   I. Gross,
Leonard.   II. Title.
GV481.C18   1986   613.7   86-11517
ISBN 0-385-19714-4

The purpose of this book is to help you gain the rejuvenating benefits of appropriate exercise while at the same time guard against the pitfalls of exercise to excess. But because movement of any kind can conceivably produce injury, it is recommended that you consult your doctor before beginning any exercise program. The instructions and advice in this or any book dealing with fitness and health should always be supplemented by your doctor's analysis of your specific condition.

To our families

CONTENTS

A NOTE FROM LEONARD GROSS

There are two extraordinary dividends a writer receives in exchange for the uncertainties and hazards of the independent life. The first of these is the freedom to come, go, and do as one pleases. The second is the ability to satisfy one's curiosity in the process of paying the bills. When a question arises for which no printed answer seems available, the writer immediately wonders if he or she is on the trail of a new book.

The question that gave rise to this book first came to mind in 1980, when my family doctor noticed a bit of sag in my posture. Although such a change was readily predictable for a person my age—I am in my fifties—particularly one who spends hours of each day with head bowed toward his work, we nonetheless agreed that this was an undesirable development I should attempt to counteract. My doctor suggested a therapy, which I immediately employed. I can't be positive that the therapy helped, but I am absolutely certain that it made me wonder whether there might be a number of special fitness strategies one could employ to reverse the effects of aging.

My desire to know about such strategies, assuming they existed, could not have been keener. Sports and fitness are major components of my life; there aren't ten days in any year that I don't play tennis or ski or have a workout. I long ago discovered that this investment of time and energy adds to my effectiveness and my ability to appreciate life. If there was a way to extend my physical effectiveness beyond the normal time span, I wanted to know about it.

There was another reason why I responded so attentively to

my doctor's suggestion. Eight years earlier, he and I had been in the midst of a torrid tennis match—in addition to being close, it was being played in ninety-degree heat—when he suddenly walked off the court to drink a quantity of water. I was shocked, and told him so. My own doctor, drinking water while exercising! Even a layperson knew better than that.

It turned out—as my doctor friend patiently explained—that *not* drinking while exercising, a staple of exercise lore since the invention of the marathon, had been exposed for the myth that it was in the period since my doctor had captained his college track team. "We know now that it's best to replace water while you exercise," he advised me.

That earlier episode had made me wonder whether there might be other unfounded myths about exercise we all assiduously observed. My research on that occasion led me to physiologist Laurence E. Morehouse at UCLA, who believed that the biggest myth of all in the realm of fitness was that you had to "kill" yourself to stay in shape. Our subsequent collaboration led to *Total Fitness,* one of the most successful books on physical conditioning ever published.

Although I am not a superstitious man, the coincidence could not escape me: The same doctor whose remark had led to *Total Fitness* had given me yet another idea for a fitness book. It was a decided spur.

Over the next several years, I amassed a foot-high file of research, but nothing I read seemed sufficiently transporting; there was no single, insightful vision that suggested a breakthrough approach to the subject of fitness and aging.

Then, in 1983, a collection of what I had supposed were sports-related afflictions led me to Dr. René Cailliet, a specialist in physical medicine who has an international reputation as a doctor-of-last-resort among persons with physiological problems that have not been resolved elsewhere. Such were my own problems that I had begun to wonder if my days as a recreational athlete were numbered.

Physical medicine is the treatment of muscular, skeletal, and neurological problems by means of exercise, heat, cold, and electricity. Of the four, exercise is the most important. Unlike orthopedic medicine, physical medicine eschews surgery in its treatment of medical problems. Surgery had already been proposed in the treatment of mine.

From the moment Dr. Cailliet walked into the examining room, my spirits began to lift. He is a hands-on doctor who draws close, grabs your arm, looks you in the eye, smiles, and says, "What's the problem?" He was, I would learn, in his mid-sixties, but as he examined me, I could see that his strength and vigor were that of a much younger man. Within the next half hour, Dr. Cailliet had persuaded me, first, that I would probably ski and play tennis for as long as I drew breath, and second, that my afflictions were related not to my sports but to the workouts I employed to put myself in shape to play them.

"Is this age-related?" I asked.

"Absolutely," he replied. "There's a point in life when heavy workouts become counterproductive." Then he said, "Do you think it would be too much of a sacrifice if you gave up jogging and took up some other activity that would give you a cardiovascular workout without damaging your body?"

"Do you think that jogging is causing my problems?"

"Absolutely."

"Then I just gave up jogging."

Following our conversation, Dr. Cailliet prescribed a series of exercises whose purpose, he said, was to counteract the effects of aging: to straighten the body, restore vital capacity, make one feel young again.

I had found my man. Then and there I told him of my idea for a book about strategies to reverse the aging process. Did the subject interest him?

"I've been doing nothing but teach and practice that subject for the last thirty-five years."

Thus was this collaboration born.

Today, my curiosity sated, I'm serene in my conviction that I've discovered the fitness strategy I'll be using for the rest of my life, one that *will* help me to live fully for as long as I draw breath. May it do as much for you.

A final note: Because this is Dr. Cailliet's story, it is written in his voice.

PART ONE

THE REJUVENATION STRATEGY

1. ON REVERSING
THE EFFECTS OF AGING

Aging is not a disease. Its manifestations can be modified. To a dramatic extent, we can not only retard the effects of aging but make ourselves younger physiologically: more flexible, more agile, more energetic, stronger—even taller.

The older we are, the more dramatic the potential for change becomes.

In later years, the biological variable in the human body can be as great as thirty years. If you have taken good care of yourself and led an active life, you can have the body and energy of a person fifteen years younger than your chronological age; conversely, if you have not cared for yourself and not led an active life, you may look and feel fifteen years older than your age. Obviously, the younger you are, the smaller the range of change. But a person of sixty can easily look forty-five—or seventy-five—and feel as though he or she is that age, too.

If you have been an inactive person for most of your life, there's little doubt that you're older-looking than you need to be, and conduct your life as though you're older than your years. People think of you as older than you are and you probably think of yourself in that way as well, dismissing new opportunities and passing up adventures because you perceive yourself as no longer having what it takes.

That condition can be swiftly reversed. The impact will be felt the first day you undertake the rejuvenation program I'll be setting forth in the succeeding chapters. Within weeks there will be a discernible change in your appearance and disposition. Within months you'll consider yourself a new person.

Lest you take these assertions for some kind of sophistry, let me present my credentials. I am the director of physical medicine and rehabilitation at Santa Monica Hospital, Santa Monica, California, and professor of medicine at the University of Southern California School of Medicine. For ten years I was chairman of that school's Department of Rehabilitative Medicine. In addition, I am the author of nine books about pain that are used as references by doctors throughout the world. Each year I give a minimum of fifty lectures to medical groups in the United States and abroad. My lectures, however technical, are always couched within the framework of the theme I'm presenting here: rejuvenation, humankind's oldest, most cherished dream, need not be a dream at all.

There is one other credential I would like to present to you in behalf of these statements. It is personal, not professional.

As these words are written, I am sixty-nine years old. Most men my age have either retired or are planning to. I have no such intention. My day begins at 5 A.M. (with a rapid one-hour walk) and ends at 11 P.M. Most of that day is given to work, which begins with hospital rounds at 7 A.M. and includes five hours of nonstop clinical practice and some combination of teaching, writing, and drawing. In the course of lecturing, I travel 200,000 miles a year, and my wife and I maintain a vigorous social and cultural life.

You would have every right to be skeptical of advice from a doctor who maintains poor health habits himself. I want to assure you, therefore, that I not only take large doses of my own prescription for youthfulness but credit it for the exhilaration I feel about life and the vigor I am able to bring to it.

Rx for a Youthful Life

What is this prescription? Essentially, it's exercise—but exercise of a special kind, exercise that comprehends the unique requirements of the aging body, employs strategies to protect and defend the body's traditional weak spots, and establishes priorities that are often ignored in traditional programs.

Where most exercise programs emphasize the development of muscles, this one—which gets to muscles eventually—begins with the body's basic building block, connective tissue.

The key to aging is what happens to tissue. A sponge that is not used dries out and withers. Unused—even underused—tissue dries out, too. Once you're thirty-five or older, your major concern ought to be to vitalize the tissues, particularly those in the more vulnerable parts of your body. That's exactly what this program does.

Where most exercise programs pay scant attention to posture, this one identifies it as the second most significant factor in maintaining a youthful body. Poor posture is the *sine qua non* of aging. When you're stooped over, you not only look old, but function that way as well. In a number of ways you probably don't even suspect, a slumping posture greatly decreases your vital capacity and your ability to move. A major objective of our program is to put you in a healthful, youthful posture, and keep you there.

Where most exercise programs are arduous, this one is so humane and realistic that many of the movements can be done while watching television or seated at your desk or sitting in your car, waiting for a light to change.

Obsessive exercising isn't necessarily healthy or desirable, and it is certainly not what 98 percent of the human race wants to do. Yet that is how exercising has been increasingly proffered over the last decade. As a consequence, it is a turnoff to most people, particularly to those past thirty-five. It seems beyond their capabilities, and strikes them as unnecessary, unpleasant, boring, and even punitive.

Most fitness programs pay only lip service to aging. They acknowledge that the older person can't and shouldn't work out as arduously as the younger one, but they offer the same basic regimens for all age groups. The fact is that conventional exercise regimens may do more harm than good to anyone past thirty-five.

When you're under thirty-five, there's almost nothing you can't do. You can run twenty, thirty, forty, even fifty miles a week. You can hyperextend in yoga and aerobics. But once you reach thirty-five, beware.

Thirty-five: The Chronological Rubicon

"Life begins at forty," the saying goes. All of us have been conditioned to think of forty as the midpoint in life. From a physiological point of view, that is actually not the case. In most of us, important changes are under way in the body by the time we reach thirty-five.

Thirty-five is certainly not aging or aged. It is the beginning, however, of what can be considered the aging process, because physiologically and functionally we start tending to deteriorate— if ever so minimally—in strength, flexibility, and physical capacity. There is an enormous variable here. People who have been extremely active up to this point will not begin to deteriorate as early or as rapidly as those who haven't. Genetics are a factor, as well; there are those with body types that are simply more durable than other body types. Nonetheless, thirty-five is the age at which we ought to be aware that changes are beginning to occur that will eventually affect our physical capacities.

As the years pass, these limitations show up to an increasing degree. Forty-five is not considered old by any means, especially not today, yet physiologically it dictates an approach to activity somewhat different from that permitted a decade earlier. And so it proceeds through the decades. By the time we reach our seventies, a certain amount of cardiovascular impairment is inevitable, which mandates a curtailment of physical activity, at least to some extent.

So yes, there is an inevitability to aging, but as the old saw has it, considering the alternatives, it's not an unpleasant prospect. Much depends on the attitude we bring to it.

During the 1984 Winter Olympics, ABC did a story about two former skiing medalists, Billy Kidd and Jimmy Huega, who also happened to be extremely close friends. Kidd admitted that he could not cope with the reality of skiing the same course each year with diminished speed. Huega, who had suffered multiple sclerosis since his championship days, considered it a miracle to be able to ski down a beginner's slope. His adversity and attitude had helped Kidd to come to terms with reality.

If we let aging get us down, we only compound the problem because we will then do nothing to hold it off for as long as possible. Far better to learn from Jimmy Huega, and consider it a miracle that we are able to do as much as we can as the years proceed.

I used to be able to do a hundred push-ups. I can't do them now. It's not something I grieve about. When I did the push-ups, it was important to me to be able to do that many. It's not important now.

To compare what you are with what you were ten, twenty, or thirty years ago is pointless. You are what you are today. Let's accept the fact that there are normal changes of aging—but not accept any more than that. Your objective should be to enjoy today as much as you can, which means to be fit and healthy—and as youthful in your appearance and activity as you can be.

A Payoff Worth the Effort

Everyone knows someone who doesn't look his or her age, or act
it. I think of my friend and colleague Jack Brody, an anesthesiolo-
gist in his seventies who plays singles at the Riviera Tennis Club
in Pacific Palisades, California. What makes Jack's game so competitive is his ability to retrieve, getting to balls that would pass
many players ten and fifteen years younger than himself.

I think of the Stroh twins, Millard and Malen, who live respec-
tively in Sacramento and Lodi, California. In the summer of his
fifty-sixth year, Millard ran a marathon one morning and played
tennis that afternoon. Malen is one of the fastest skiers at Mt.
Reba in Bear Valley, California.

I think of Sue Garratt of San Mateo, California, who in 1982
successfully competed in Hawaii's Iron Man triathlon, swimming
2.5 miles, bicycling 112 miles, and running a marathon all in the
space of seventeen hours and thirty-two minutes. At the time, Sue
was forty-four.

To a certain extent, feats like these can be attributed to the
genetic gifts bestowed at birth. Some people are fortunate to be
of a neurophysiological muscle type that makes it possible for
them to be the superior athletes they are. That's a fact of life all of
us must confront. Thousands of children are given violins, but
only a few become a Zuckerman, a Perlman, or a Heifitz. It's the
same with physical development.

But no one, no matter how gifted, can progress unless development takes place. The kind of extravagant youthfulness I've just
cited is due to more than just genetics; to a great extent, it's the
yield of an active life. It's physical activity that slows down and
even reverses the effects of aging—an acknowledgment given
prominent display by the New York *Times* in a June 1986 article by
Jane E. Brody. The first three paragraphs of that article summa-
rize the case succinctly:

"Researchers are finding that moderate exercise can not only retard the effects of aging but can actually reverse them.

"Proper exercise, appropriately and carefully pursued throughout life . . . has been shown in scores of studies to significantly deter the deterioration of bodily functions that traditionally accompany aging.

"Among the demonstrated benefits are increased work capacity, improved heart and respiratory function, lower blood pressure, increased muscle strength, denser bones, greater flexibility, quicker reaction times, clearer thinking and reduced susceptibility to depression."

Will physical activity enable you to live longer as well? Doctors and physiologists have disputed this point for years, but until recently there has been no evidence to settle it. In March 1986, however, the *New England Journal of Medicine* published the results of a benchmark study indicating that regular, moderate exercise *does* prolong life.

The study was based on data collected from nearly 17,000 alumni of Harvard University whose ages at the start of the study ranged from thirty-five to seventy-four. The data was compiled between the mid-1960s and 1978. "Alumni mortality rates were significantly lower among the physically active," Dr. Ralph S. Paffenbarger, Jr., of Stanford University, who directed the study, reported. Some of the conclusions:

• Those men who exercised regularly reduced their risk of dying from major diseases.

• Those men with hypertension who exercised regularly reduced their death rate by half.

• Regular exercise reduced mortality rates 25 percent among men either or both of whose parents died before the age of sixty-five, and 50 percent among men whose parents lived beyond sixty-five.

• The more a man exercised, the better his longevity prospects. Among men who walked nine or more miles a week, the mortality rate was 21 percent lower than among men who walked three miles or less. Among men who engaged in light sports one or two hours a week, life expectancy was 24 percent greater than among those who did nothing.

The results of that study are a powerful inducement for a physically active life. While men only were included in the study, it is a fair conjecture that when a similar study is undertaken with women the results will be the same.

No one, of course, can *guarantee* that your time on earth will be extended if you exercise. But, at a minimum, living a healthy life can certainly enhance your chances of avoiding premature death. And your ability to live in a youthful spirit and with a more youthful body is definitely within your power. The Rejuvenation Strategy, simply put, is the process by which you convert aging tissue into a healthier, more youthful state.

Obviously, if you've never exercised at all, you're not going to obtain the longevity benefits or be the person you might have been if you'd been exercising all your life. If you're at 1 or 2 on a scale of 10, you probably won't reach 9 or 10. But you can easily rise to 7 or even 8—truly a life-changing improvement.

Here's a typical story, told to me by the wife of a friend:

"George had always avoided exercise. Positively hated it. He wasn't all that good at sports, so he avoided those, too. By the time he was fifty, he weighed 20 percent more than he did when we were married and, well, frankly, something had gone out of the marriage. It wasn't that I didn't love him. I did. But there was a vitality missing. He seemed older than he was. I don't think I had unrealistic expectations, but we were the same age, and I, who had always remained active, just had a lot more energy than he did. About a year ago, for reasons I'll never understand, George decided to change his ways. He suddenly became very careful about the things he was eating and drinking. And he embarked on an exercise program that included a long walk at a rapid pace every morning. Today, I have the feeling that I'm once again living with the man I married."

If you've never been an active person, even the mildest exercise regimen might seem forbidding at first. But very quickly, your own feedback will carry you across this psychological threshold. You'll know from experience that a reward awaits you, a feeling of well-being more than worth whatever you've done to get it.

If you are an active person, you already know firsthand about the glowing feeling that nothing but exercise can give you. What you may not know—but will after you've finished this book—is how and why your present workouts could be causing you serious, even permanent damage.

"No Pain, No Gain": An Idea Whose Time Has Gone

The last decade has been marked by an intense preoccupation with health. Millions of Americans have stopped smoking because of indications that the habit can lead to lung cancer, heart disease, and other problems. In April 1984, the American Cancer Society reported that per capita consumption of cigarettes dropped 7 percent in 1983, the largest drop ever recorded in a single year. Similarly, many Americans have cut down on their intake of beef and dairy products because of the correlation between cholesterol intake and heart attacks. They have become wary of salt, sugar, preservatives, and other additions to diet. And finally, many of these same people have turned to exercise.

It is now a dozen years since the onset of the fitness craze. There is no sign of a letup; if anything, interest has intensified. Parks and streets are filled with runners. Advertisements push exercise equipment and fitness centers, and anyone who patronizes those centers knows how crowded they can be. A few years ago, the Los Angeles *Times* did a long article about fitness in the business world, stating: "They're doing leg lifts at the IRS. Pelvic tilts at Getty Oil. Jumping jacks at the Beverly Hilton. Side lunges at the FBI . . . and more. That the fitness craze is hitting business and government hard is being demonstrated daily in company cafeterias, employee lounges and conference rooms, all of which are being transformed into part time fitness centers."

As a physician who has devoted his life to physical medicine, I should be very happy about these developments. The fact is that I disapprove of much of what is going on.

By and large, the increasing awareness of fitness has produced salutary effects. Figures indicate that heart problems have diminished among Americans, and researchers are willing to credit an emphasis on exercise and diet. But in the process we have all been brainwashed into believing that we must run twenty miles a week or bend ourselves into pretzels in order to stay in shape. Not only are such efforts unnecessary, they can easily produce debilitating injuries.

The assumption underlying a great deal of the fitness boom is that if a little bit of exercise is a good thing, a great deal of exercise should be that much better. That is simply not the case. At a certain point, it is very much against your interests to work out as hard as you can, no matter how good it may feel at the moment.

It's not just a matter of being unable to do as much as we age as we could when we were younger. It's that trying to do as much, or nearly as much, does us no good—and probably causes harm. That is the unmistakable message recent experience is giving us.

Over the last decade—a period that coincides with the fitness boom—it has become increasingly apparent that something is radically wrong with the manner in which many Americans are going about the process of getting fit. During that period, the number of fitness-related injuries has escalated dramatically.

A dozen years is not a long time from a scientific point of view. Nonetheless, significant figures are beginning to appear suggesting that a certain percentage of persons have been injured as a consequence of violent exercise who otherwise might not have been injured. And within the medical profession the impression is overwhelming that such injuries have vastly increased. Not a week goes by that I don't see a minimum of three new patients suffering from exercise-induced injuries. Significantly, nine out of ten of these patients are thirty-five years old or older. Many other doctors, numbers of them in the field of physical medicine, have reported similar experiences.

In making this statement, I am not relying on articles in medical journals or on hearsay. Because I lecture so frequently to medical groups throughout the United States, as well as abroad, I have a vast network of informants not available to most other doctors. If what these people report to me during question-and-answer sessions and at informal meetings after my lectures is any indication, then exercise-related injuries have reached epidemic proportions.

I want to make it very clear that I'm not speaking of injuries incurred while playing sports. I am speaking of injuries incurred while trying to get in shape. What an irony that is! It's almost as though the injured would have been better off not doing anything at all.

Of course that's not the case. The person who doesn't exercise at all is damaging his or her body just as surely as the person who is overextending it. Inactivity rapidly deconditions the body; for every week that you go without exercise, you have lost 10 percent of your fitness. You need only think of the last time you were bedridden to reassure yourself on this point. Only some of the weakness you felt on finally arising was due to your illness; the rest was the consequence of inactivity.

All sorts of things happen to muscles that aren't used, and all of them are bad. It's blood that carries nourishment to the body parts; it's exercise that moves the blood. When you don't exercise sufficiently, an insufficient supply of blood reaches the muscles. When you don't exercise at all, the supply of blood is dangerously diminished. Blood transports oxygen and calcium, both necessary to the muscle's health. When the supply of these two necessities is drastically reduced, the muscle fiber loses bulk just as surely as you would lose weight if your food supply were cut off. Tendons and ligaments become more fragile, as well. I repeat: If you're not exercising, you're courting disaster.

We've said that the right kind of activity can rejuvenate your body. Let's now state the obverse. If you exercise improperly, you can age your body just as surely as if you hadn't exercised at all. If you're thirty-five and you exercise as though you're twenty-five, you can wind up feeling forty-five just as surely as if you hadn't done a thing. That, alas, is what seems to be happening to increasing numbers of people.

Throughout America today, crimes against the body are being committed in the name of fitness. Perfectly healthy recreational athletes are cutting their playing time by years, even decades. With the best of intentions, they have heeded an abundance of advice from dubious sources and pushed and strained their bodies with no understanding whatever about what's going on under their skin.

"No pain, no gain," the exercise addicts tell you. That may be true for competitive bodybuilders and athletes who need to accustom themselves to the extreme exertion required in their sports. It is almost never true for recreational athletes, and it is absolutely never true for anyone past thirty-five.

Taking Charge of Your Own Development

In the last decade, along with the fitness boom, there has been a great heightening of awareness among lay people about their responsibility for their own health care. Increasingly, they demand an active role. Among physicians, it's expected now that the intelligent patient will not only want to know but *demand* to know about the consequences of treatment and the side effects of medicine. Does it not follow that if a sensible person shouldn't take medication without inquiring about side effects, a prescription for exercise shouldn't be taken on faith either?

If you exercise at all, you owe it to yourself to discover exactly what's going to happen to you as a consequence of going through a series of unusual movements and enduring abnormal stress.

The older you are, the more imperative it becomes for you to know what's going on inside your body.

To achieve that objective, I'm going to do something that, to the best of my knowledge, has never been done before in a book about fitness for the general public. I'm going to show you exactly what happens to your body, first, when you stress it in a dangerous way, and second, when you exercise it beneficially.

You'll learn how to analyze your body to determine whether certain arduous exercise programs such as jogging are a good idea for you—or whether you'd be well advised to substitute a less injury-prone activity.

You'll also learn:

- How to rejuvenate aging tissue.
- How to make a simple postural adjustment that will make you look and feel younger—and probably make you taller.
- How to regain lost strength, to the point that you're almost as strong as you were a decade before.
- How to defend the most vulnerable parts of your body from injury and the encroachments of age.
- How to walk your way to fitness.
- How to relax.
- How to stabilize your weight, or lose weight, while eating ingredients designed to keep you young.
- How to hold on to the youthfulness you regain.

My message, in a nutshell, is this: The right kind of conditioning program will rejuvenate your body. The wrong kind could cripple it. Let's deal with the problems first, and then devote ourselves to the possibilities.

2. THE TROUBLE WITH STRENUOUS EXERCISE

Not long ago, I spent an afternoon in a popular gym on the west side of Los Angeles. Although it was during working hours, the floor was filled with men and women, mostly in their late twenties and thirties. Every machine was in constant use. What I saw appalled me. Not one of these people was exercising in a manner that didn't pose at least some kind of danger to his or her body. As they strained to push or pull the weights, they almost invariably arched their backs, an absolute no-no we'll be exploring in a moment. Often they would jerk the weights, a movement that can damage spinal disks as well as muscles and ligaments. And all of them, without exception, appeared to accept without question the idea central to the Holy Writ of the fitness movement—that if it isn't hurting, it can't be helping.

The companion to this notion is the die-hard myth that the last repetition of any exercise, the one you strain your gut to perform, is the one that does you the most good. That myth, like so many others associated with the fitness-through-torture school, is a bunch of nonsense. The truth is that the first repetition of any exercise is at least as beneficial as the last, and a good bit less dangerous. On the first repetition your muscles are fresh; on the last they are fatigued. Food stores have been depleted, and the muscles have filled with accumulations of lactic acid, the waste products of previous contractions. Add to this the loss of form by bodybuilders as they strain to make that last repetition, and you've got a classic condition for serious damage to tissue.

On the floor of this gym were several men and women doing a

series of supposedly beneficial stretching exercises half a dozen of which were guaranteed to do them considerable harm and absolutely no good. A few feet away was a chart detailing instructions on how to perform the very same injury-inducing movements.

Each morning on my way to work I cross a boulevard you have probably seen dozens of times in films. It is a six-lane boulevard with a broad, grassy divider in the middle graced by a single line of coral trees strung out in a line from the palisades at the end of Santa Monica to a point three miles inland. As you can imagine, the grassy strip is an extremely popular jogging path; on any given morning scores of joggers are using it. During the several months that I have been working on this manuscript, I have made a special point of stopping to observe the joggers.

From an orthopedic point of view, a majority of those I observed should not be jogging at all. For them, serious, perhaps permanent injury is inescapable.

Let me put the case as conservatively as I can, given the experience of the last decade. Sixty to seventy-five percent of joggers are going to wind up with foot, ankle, hip, or back problems, or a combination of two or more problems. Those are truly terrible numbers. They become even more terrible when you substitute real people for percentages. I think of two recent cases. The first was a superbly conditioned jogger in his fifties who was also an outstanding athlete, one of those people who play every sport with grace. His great passion was skiing, to the point that he had programmed a gradual reduction in his workload each year so that he could ski the great mountains of Europe, North America, and even South America. But just when he got himself in a financial position secure enough to realize his dream, he developed a serious and painful condition in his knee—almost certainly caused by jogging—to the point that he couldn't ski at all. Unfortunately, even the most advanced surgical techniques have failed to restore his knee to anything like the condition it was in before jogging ruined it.

The second case involved a lovely woman just approaching

fifty, lean, stately, alert, outgoing. When she first came to me with a knee problem, I asked her to stop jogging, and gave her a series of exercises. But the damage was too extensive; her knee did not respond. On subsequent visits, she reported that she could no longer dance and went up and down stairs with difficulty. "I'm devastated," she said. "Not only am I being denied the pleasure of the activities I enjoy, I'm not able to exercise normally to stay fit."

Had these two people not exercised so strenuously in the past, they would, in all likelihood, have avoided the predicament they find themselves in today. Both are extremely intelligent people; had they had the slightest warning, they might have eased off enough to prevent permanent injury. But in both cases, the damage was insidious. It happens all the time with injuries such as these. For a long time, you feel nothing untoward, no pain, no discomfort, no loss of function. But gradually, the body parts wear down until, all of a sudden, movement *is* difficult and painful —and by then it's too late to remedy the damage.

One of the greatest problems with strenuous exercise is precisely here: You often aren't aware of the damage you're producing until you've produced it. To the contrary, all the signals tell you that you're doing your body a great favor. When you're jogging, for example, you often feel wonderful. You get a high that decreases the very sensations designed to trigger alarms. (The high is an endocrine response to exercise, in which the adrenal glands enlarge and secrete a morphine-like substance. In extreme cases, some inveterate runners literally become addicted; they will punish themselves and abuse their bodies to work off their addiction and get the high that they can't get in any other legal way.) The bout of exercises is followed by a tremendous sense of well-being and an increase in energy. You look better, too, because people who exercise glow.

There's no doubt whatever that jogging benefits the cardiovascular system. But this benefit has to be weighed against the profound muscular and skeletal deterioration that so often results. There *are* those persons fortunate enough to be able to jog without injury. For them, jogging is often extraordinarily pleasurable as well as physically beneficial. I would certainly never proscribe jogging for them. But as we'll see further on, such people are in the minority. Most of us can't get away with it.

If you're a jogger thirty-five years old or older and you've never experienced difficulty, you may well be one of the fortunate ones. But it may also be possible that undetected and unfelt damage is under way in your body. Not even X rays may be able to identify the deterioration in your low back, hip joints, knees, and ankles.

I've singled out jogging because it has become such a tremendously popular form of exercise over the last decade. But the problems we're discussing apply to any form of exercise that places an unnatural stress on joints and tissue. There are many problems, but basically they boil down to just two.

Weight Bearing: A Case of "More Is Less"

First, a bit of simple anatomy:

A joint is composed of two bones that come together for the purpose of movement.

The end of every bone is covered with a cushioning substance known as *cartilage*. Cartilage can be considered part of the bone because it is inherently connected to it. But it is made of a different substance.

Bone is solid. It has no compressibility. Cartilage, on the other hand, is semifluid, 80 percent water, a Jell-O-like substance that is very spongy.

Cartilage performs two vital functions. First, it absorbs the shock of compression when any kind of weight is placed upon the joint. The knee, hip, and ankle joints experience such compression when you walk or run, but also when you simply stand. Second, cartilage secretes a lubricant whenever it is squeezed by a compressing force. It's this oil that lubricates the joint and enables the two parts to move together without causing wear and tear and pain. Left to itself, the fluid would make its way through other parts of the body. It's kept where it belongs by a capsule, somewhat like a rubber container, that girdles the joint.

Once the squeezing stops, the cartilage expands and sucks the fluid back in, just like a compressed sponge in water returning to its normal shape. That action of compression and relaxation is what keeps the cartilage healthy.

It's the cartilage and the lubricant secreted by the cartilage that causes the joints to function swiftly and painlessly. Without the cartilage and its lubricant, you'd have bone rubbing against bone, an unimaginably painful circumstance.

As we age, however, the cartilage begins to wear out in several ways. First, it dehydrates, just like the rest of our tissue. Second, it develops microscopic fractures—tiny slits no wider than a human hair—mostly as a consequence of weight bearing. These miniscule breaks tend to weaken the cartilage and produce other breaks. In such fashion does the cartilage dry, crack, and shrink over the years, and as it does, the fit between the two bones becomes rough, instead of smooth as it once was. The process is inevitable and irreversible; the trick is to confine it to a minimum and retard its rate.

The key to that result is how much weight we bear, and the manner in which we bear it.

Weight bearing is unavoidable. It need not be detrimental. It can even be desirable. Only when it's excessive does it become a problem.

Cartilage covers the ends of all bones that form joints. It is made of a spongy substance and acts like a sponge, absorbing shock and secreting a fluid that lubricates the joints. As weight-bearing pressure squeezes the cartilage, juice flows out of it and into the joint. When the weight-bearing pressure is released, the cartilage sucks the fluid back in.

CARTILAGE

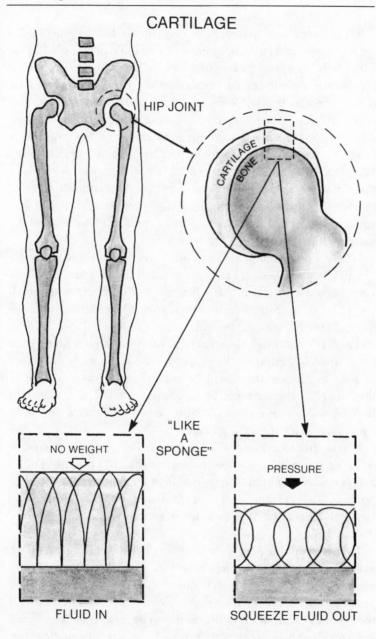

HIP JOINT

CARTILAGE
BONE

"LIKE A SPONGE"

NO WEIGHT

PRESSURE

FLUID IN

SQUEEZE FLUID OUT

Some years ago, I treated a man in his forties who had a splendid physique, a consequence of years of daily weight lifting, using weights in some cases in excess of three hundred pounds. He did not come to see me because he was experiencing pain; he was concerned because over the years he had become increasingly stiff. As I examined him, I discovered that his impression was correct; his spine was about as flexible as a bamboo rod.

The spine consists of approximately thirty vertebrae, which are separated by disks. These disks act like cushions, just as cartilage does, and are actually a form of cartilage. By constantly subjecting his spinal disks to such inordinate pressures, this man had squeezed the juice out of all of them, until they were approximately 20 percent of their normal size.

When you're young, you can lift heavy weights and probably get away with it, because at that age all of the building blocks of your body are intact, in particular the billion fibers with which you're born. By thirty-five, however, you've lost millions of those fibers through attrition, and will continue to lose millions more as you age. It's as though the structural supports in your home have diminished in girth over the years; the house is simply no longer as solid as it once was. Cartilage is particularly vulnerable after thirty-five, as the example of my patient attests; undue weight bearing will squeeze fluid out of it just as surely as if you were squeezing water out of a sponge.

What qualifies as "undue"? For a man of average size thirty-five or older, it would be any weight heavier than 125 pounds. For an average-sized woman thirty-five or older, it would be 100 pounds. Larger men and women could lift correspondingly larger weights. The best measure is a subjective one: If it hurts, it's too heavy.

That rule applies, regardless of age, because lifting excessive amounts of weight at any age is bad for you. The payment is too great for the benefit—which is questionable to begin with. Most people who exercise with weights do so for cosmetic reasons; they're only incidentally concerned with becoming strong. There *is* a correlation between strength and the size of muscles, but even young bodybuilders overdo it, bulking themselves up to such enormous proportions that they have far more strength than they can use.

There is no question that young people are abusing themselves today with extremely stressful activities that lay the groundwork for future physical breakdown. Such breakdown can produce defects that can't be overcome, and those who suffer them will have to curtail their activities for the rest of their lives.

You're a Weight Lifter, Too—Whether You Know It or Not

Along about this point, two questions may have come to mind. The first might be, "If weight lifting presents so many potential problems, shouldn't it be avoided altogether?" Not at all. Done sensibly, it can firm the body, replacing fat with muscle, and give you added strength and endurance. Lifting sensibly means diminishing the amount of weight you use in any given exercise as you age, and increasing the number of repetitions. As long as it feels good and it's done right, weight lifting is fine.

The second question you may be asking at this point is, "How does all this apply to me? I'm no weight lifter." Not true. We are all weight lifters—to a degree that has important implications for cartilage.

When you stand, you're duplicating to a very small degree exactly what went on in the back of that man with the semirigid spine. Any amount of weight on the joints squeezes the cartilage, secreting juice into the joints, just as it's designed to do. If you're overweight, you're putting an extra squeeze on your cartilage just as surely as if you were holding a weight overhead equal to your extra poundage. And whenever you're active, the pressure increases as well—*in proportion to the intensity of your activity.*

If 100 pounds of body weight are bearing down on your hips,

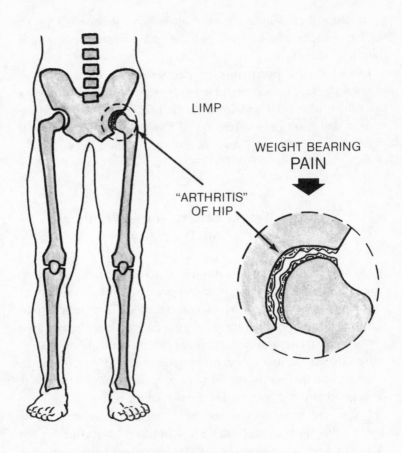

LIMP

WEIGHT BEARING
PAIN

"ARTHRITIS"
OF HIP

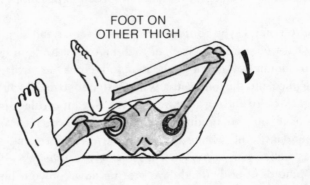

FOOT ON
OTHER THIGH

knees, and ankles when you're standing, 400 pounds are bearing down when you walk, and 800 to 900 pounds when you jog. The cartilage is built to take the walking. It *needs* the walking. What it doesn't need and cannot take is the pounding and grinding inflicted on it 900 times a mile whenever you jog. If you're an overweight jogger, the damage is that much worse.

Here's what happens. The weight and force flatten the cartilage against the bones to the point that there is almost no cartilage to serve as a buffer between them. The weight need not be excessive to cause damage; if it is applied in an abrupt or violent manner, that's usually enough to cause the cartilage to fracture into those hair-thin lines. Once that happens, fluid leaks away. Before you know it, the cartilage has shrunk. Once smooth, glistening, and slippery, able to glide across the surface of its mate, the cartilage has now developed a wavy surface, with valleys in between the peaks. The surface, moreover, tends to be dry, as the cartilage loses its capacity to secrete lubricating fluids. Movement, once effortless, becomes increasingly painful. Healthy cartilage tissue has no nerves and is therefore free of pain. But once fractures develop, they mend with fibrous tissue, and fibrous tissue—also known as scar tissue—*does* have nerves and *can* produce pain.

Here's an example of what happens when cartilage fractures as a consequence of excessive weight bearing. The once-smooth surfaces in the hip socket are now jagged. Movement produces pain. You begin to walk with a limp.

To test for arthritis of the hip: **1.** Lie on the floor. **2.** Place your left foot on your right thigh, then push your left leg as far as it will go. **3.** Repeat with the other leg.

If the movement is equal in both limbs, you're presently without problems. But if the motion of one leg is more limited, or if the movement produced any pain, it could be a sign of degenerative arthritis.

That painful condition I've just described is called "degenerative arthritis." While it's often hereditary, the disease also occurs when you don't exercise enough, or when you exercise too much.

Next, let's look at the other major anatomical problem associated with too strenuous exercise.

Stretching: "More Is Less," Part Two

Our bones are held together at their joints by *ligaments*. These ligaments are located outside the balloonlike container that encases the joint and retains its fluid.

Ligaments not only hold the bones together, but also guide them in their movements, somewhat like checkreins on a horse. A horse wearing checkreins can turn his head and neck only so far; in a similar fashion, our ligaments keep us from bending our limbs any farther than we should.

Ligaments are made of tissue. All tissue, like all matter, has a limit to which it can be stretched. Beyond that point it tears, and eventually it breaks.

All joints have a normal "range of motion." They will bend no farther than the ligaments permit. Bend a joint beyond its natural limit and the ligaments will tear.

What determines this "natural limit"? There are two major factors. The first is heredity.

Body types have different characteristics. Some people are simply more flexible than others. Their joints are constructed in a manner that permits them a greater range of motion. Their tissue is more elastic as well. The best artistic dancers are born with a suppleness that is simply not acquirable. A person born without such genetic flexibility who is trained almost from infancy can close the gap to an extent but will never be a world-class dancer no matter how hard he or she works.

The second major factor affecting flexibility is the familiar one of age.

Bend a young, green twig almost double and it won't tear or break. Bend an old, dried-out twig like that and you'll snap it in two. The lesson applies to us.

When we're young, our ligamentous structures are tremendously flexible. They also recover quickly from great stress and strain, such as that experienced in a competition. A well-conditioned athlete can be back on the playing field a day or two after an all-out game. The older we get, the longer it takes to recuperate and the more danger there is of injury. Our tissues no longer have the tensile strength they once did; they have lost a certain amount of their capacity to be stretched. They are less moist, and more fragile. When they're overstretched, they respond like an old, dried-out rubber band.

Stretching is absolutely essential to the maintenance of a healthy and youthful body. Stretching becomes bad for you when you stretch your tissues beyond their normal anatomical capabilities. You can do that only by overstretching and tearing them. Rather than assisting you, that kind of stretching damages the tissues and makes them age faster. Stretching should never make you sore, let alone lame.

When an exercise is uncomfortable and producing pain, it's going to cause aching of a greater intensity and for a longer duration than you would ever expect. That discomfort you feel is nature saying "no." Contrary to the "no pain, no gain" dictum that has gained such currency in recent years, the discomfort may well be an indication that your joints and tissues may not be made to do what you're asking of them. Rather than "working through" pain or injury, you're simply going to aggravate the condition.

When one tries an exercise that is very difficult, the suggestion is often made that "you'll get used to it." If the exercise is difficult for you simply because you're out of condition, then you will get used to it. But if it's difficult because you're not made for it, you'll never get used to it. No one gets used to pain—and you will never get less pain by attempting to push your limbs beyond the point they're meant to go, or bending beyond your capacity to do so.

There's a limit to every joint's range of motion; the only way you can exceed it is by tearing tissue.

We are not all born with equal flexibility. We are not all able to put our palms on the floor without bending our knees. We are not all able to arch our backs and touch our heads to the floor. What's more, it is not of any particular advantage to be able to perform either feat.

If you are normally supple, it is of absolutely no advantage for you to be more supple still. The whole reason for flexibility is to be certain that every joint can move to the degree it should to maintain normal function. To be still more flexible not only is useless, but can produce another category of problems. The only way you can increase your suppleness beyond natural limits is to overstretch your tissues. What then supports your joints?

Every joint is surrounded by "connective tissue"—ligaments, capsule, and tendons. That girdle has to have enough stretch in it to permit the joint to move in an efficient manner. The moment the girdle loses its elasticity, the moment it's stretched too far, the joint it's encasing becomes floppy and unstable.

Undue stretching endangers muscles as well.

Ligaments hold your bones together. Muscles move the bones. (They are fastened to them by tendons.) Every muscle is like a hot dog with a skin. It's not the muscle that stretches, it's the skin in which it's encased. The fibers in that casement—known as "collagen"—can be examined under a microscope, and they are wondrous to behold: exquisitely engineered three-threaded springs. Like any spring, they can only stretch so far; beyond a certain point, they won't recoil to their normal shape; beyond that point they'll break. Result: a painful pulled muscle at best, and possibly permanent damage.

Rule: Stretch only so far and for so long as it feels good. The instant you feel discomfort, pull back or stop.

"X-Rated" Exercises

Let's illustrate the hazards of overstretching with one of the simplest, most popular—and potentially most hazardous—exercises of all: touching the toes.

There are physicians who will tell you that if you can't touch your toes without bending your knees, you're not fit. I think that's absolute nonsense. I've examined thousands of extremely well-conditioned patients—men in particular—who can't readily touch their toes simply because they are naturally inflexible in the muscles and joints involved in that particular exercise. I would certainly never recommend that they try to develop the capacity, because bending over in such a manner can lead to a painful injury, particularly if you're over thirty-five.

The older we become, the more we have to stretch in order to touch fingers to toes. But what exactly are we stretching? Two major muscle groups are involved: the hamstrings, which are located behind the thigh, and the back muscles. The problem is that the hamstrings, as a rule, aren't all that flexible and don't stretch very much. If you've bent over and still aren't touching your toes, all the further bending you do to reach your goal is done at the expense of the back. Result: a pulled, or over-stretched muscle and chronic lower back pain.

Touching the toes is only one of many potentially harmful exercises—*Esquire* called them "X-rated" in the June 1984 issue—performed hundreds of thousands of times each day in aerobics and yoga classes, as well as in homes, throughout the United States and much of the Western world.

The basic problem with these classes and the exercises they espouse is a conceptual one. They appear to function on a variation of the premise that if a little bit of exercise is good for you, a great deal of it would be that much better. Flexibility is a very good example of why this isn't necessarily so.

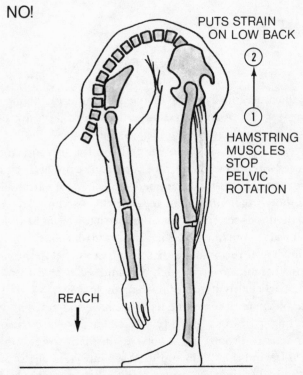

NO!

PUTS STRAIN
ON LOW BACK

② ↑ ①

HAMSTRING
MUSCLES
STOP
PELVIC
ROTATION

REACH ↓

Here's why touching your toes with your knees locked can be harmful. The hamstring muscles don't stretch much; at a certain point they stop your pelvis from rotating. From then on, it's your low back muscles that must stretch. When you're young, you can get away with it; after thirty-five, watch out.

There is no question that yoga postures as well as the stretching exercises done in aerobics classes increase flexibility. But they may increase it too much. When the tissue that holds joints in place is stretched too much, it loses its elasticity and the joints can pop out.

But even when these exercises are performed in moderation,

OK

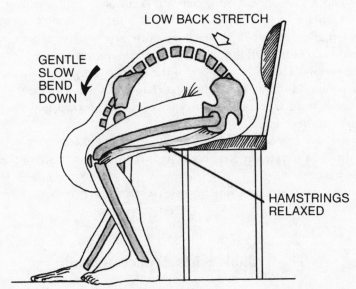

If you want to stretch your low back, here's a safe way to do it.

they represent a hazard because of the positions in which they put the body. Here are the other "X-rated" positions:

• Any exercise that begins with both legs straight in front of you and requires you to bend forward or backward at the waist. Attempting to touch the toes while seated on the floor would be an example of a bending-forward exercise; a straight-legged sit-up would involve both forward and backward bending from the waist. In all such movements you're putting an unnecessary strain on the lower back.

• Any exercise in which you hyperflex your knee. Deep knee bends, full squats, duck walks, and the so-called hurdler's stretch, in which you tuck one shin under the thigh while you stretch the other leg forward—all of these stretch the ligaments in the knee beyond any usefulness, and often tear them, and can also damage the cartilage.

Hyperflexion also damages the menisci, two cartilages on the inside and outside of the knee that fill in the vacant spaces of the knee joints. The main purpose of the menisci is to lubricate the knee joint. More on that in the next chapter; for now, it's enough to understand that if the menisci are damaged and crushed, they can't do their job.

• Any exercise in which you lift your straightened legs together while lying on your back. Again, possible damage to the low back.

• Any exercise in which you excessively arch your back.

The Trouble with Hyperextension

There is a current school of thought, originating from Australia and New Zealand, which holds that arching the back is an excellent practice. To offset the damage caused by the common bent-over forward posture, this argument holds, we must bend in the opposite direction.

I thoroughly agree that a slumping posture overstretches tissue. But I will never concede that one can undo damage by causing further damage—which is precisely what hyperflexion of the spine will do.

A mild amount of lordosis—curvature of the spine—is physiologically normal. A certain amount of hyperextension—excessive arching of the back—is inevitable in both exercise and sports and won't hurt you. If you're a tennis player, for example, it would be pretty difficult for you to hit a proper serve without arching your back. But arching to excess frequently and deliberately, as called for in many popular workouts, will inevitably cause wear and tear

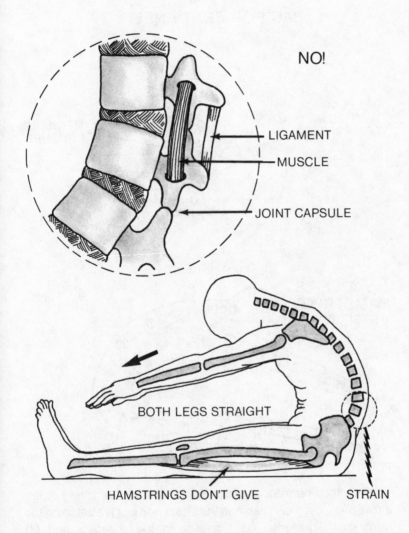

NO!

LIGAMENT

MUSCLE

JOINT CAPSULE

BOTH LEGS STRAIGHT

HAMSTRINGS DON'T GIVE   STRAIN

Stretching both hamstrings at the same time, whether you're standing or on the floor, is a risky proposition. There are six hamstring muscles that do not normally stretch, which means that all stretching is ultimately imposed upon the low back, unduly taxing muscles, ligaments, joints, and even disk tissues in that area.

BAD FOR BENT KNEE

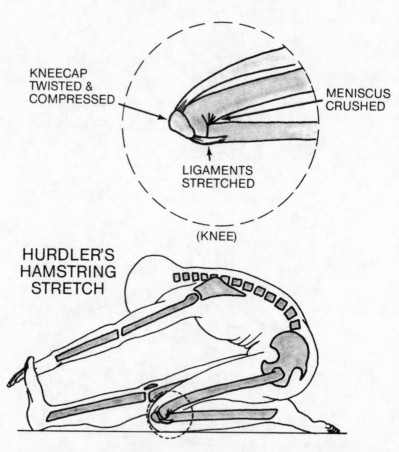

KNEECAP
TWISTED &
COMPRESSED

MENISCUS
CRUSHED

LIGAMENTS
STRETCHED

(KNEE)

HURDLER'S HAMSTRING STRETCH

The hurdler's hamstring stretch will stretch the hamstring of the straight leg, but it can damage the bent knee by (1) stretching the front knee ligaments, (2) side-slipping the kneecap, and (3) crushing the rear portion of the meniscus.

AVOID DEEP KNEE BENDS

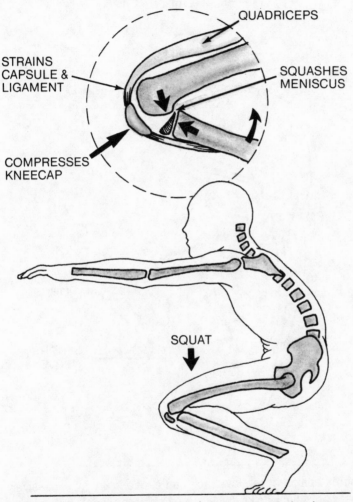

Deep knee bends endanger the ligaments of the knee, and squash the meniscus. They also compress the kneecap. Partial knee bends, which strengthen the thigh muscles and strengthen the heel cords, are okay.

ARCH OK
HYPERARCH NOT OK

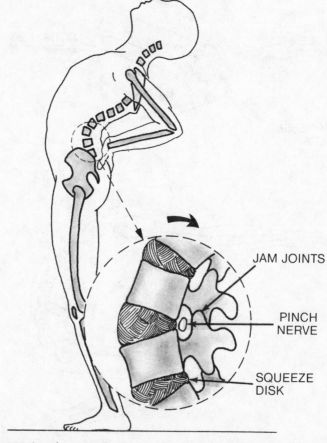

JAM JOINTS

PINCH
NERVE

SQUEEZE
DISK

Hyperextension of the low back can cause injury by excessively squeezing spinal disks (which resemble cartilage), by jamming together the spinal joints, and by pinching the nerve fibers that emerge from the spinal windows to form the sciatic nerve.

DANGEROUS

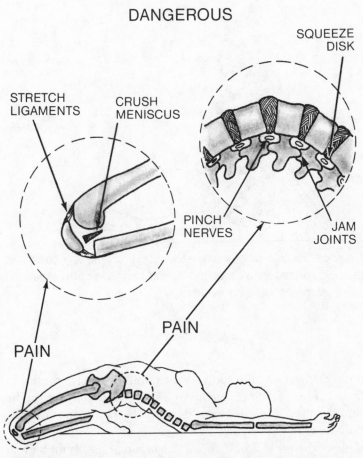

Advocates of this stretching position consider it an ultimate test of suppleness. That it may be, but it's also fraught with dangers, overstretching some tissues, crushing others, pinching nerves, and jamming joints. Great for ballet dancers and Olympic gymnasts perhaps (although they'll probably pay for their gyrations eventually), but of dubious value for the rest of us at any age; to be avoided at all costs once you're thirty-five or older.

AVOID

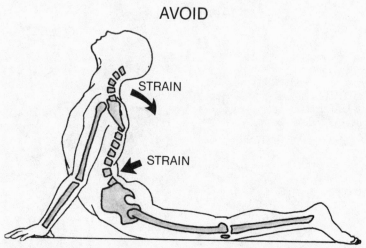

STRAIN

STRAIN

This yoga position places excessive strain on the low back and the neck, endangering disks, joints, and nerves in both places. All such positions should be avoided.

on the cartilages of the spine—which, unfortunately, are few in number. These cartilages are located in the posterior joints of the spine; as they begin to wear down pain results and arthritic changes set in.

One of the great problems with yoga is that it calls for a great deal of hyperextension. While there is much in yoga that is helpful, increasing the arch of the back excessively not only causes wear and tear, but can jam the joints of the back together and pinch the roots of the sciatic nerve.

One of the great problems with weight lifting, which has become such a popular form of conditioning in recent years, is that so many of the exercises almost force you to hyperextend the back. Several examples are shown in the accompanying illustrations. If you are using Nautilus equipment to build your body, I suggest you make every effort to ascertain that you are not hyper-

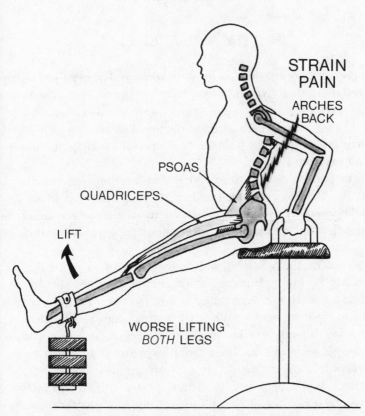

STRESSFUL

STRAIN
PAIN

ARCHES
BACK

PSOAS

QUADRICEPS

LIFT

WORSE LIFTING
BOTH LEGS

This exercise, in which both legs pull up simultaneously against resistance, might be safe if done one leg at a time. It rarely is. As the quadricep contracts, so does the psoas, or hip flexor muscle, which pulls the spine forward, arching the lower back. Result: strain and pain.

extending your low back. The best way to do that is to use lighter weights. Lowering the head or bending the knees, where appropriate, is also helpful.

The Bottom Line

There are people who can exercise strenuously, even violently, throughout their lives and never wear out their body parts. Most of us aren't like that; if we exercise too strenuously after the age of thirty-five, we greatly increase the likelihood that we'll experience serious, perhaps permanent injury. Our body parts simply can't take the strain.

The point is not that everyone must abandon strenuous exercise. It's that not everyone can do it, and therefore should not do it. The problem today is that millions of people *are* doing it regardless of whether their bodies are capable of withstanding the strain.

If you're thirty-five or older, this doesn't mean that you shouldn't exercise. It means, at a minimum, that you should not be doing what you were doing before the age of thirty-five, or what people younger than thirty-five are doing. You should not be doing the same exercises week after week, month after month as the person who's ten, twenty, or thirty years younger than you.

Having heard the case against too strenuous exercise for persons thirty-five or older, let us now consider the evidence that little or no exercise at all can cause as much or greater damage.

Exercises to strengthen and enlarge the trapezius and latissimus dorsi muscles have little but cosmetic value. They do, however, force you to increase the arch of the low back as the weight being pulled increases. The neck is also arched in a potentially harmful manner.

DANGEROUS AND USELESS

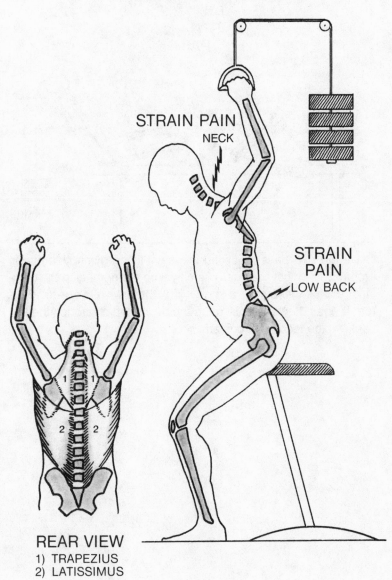

STRAIN PAIN
NECK

STRAIN
PAIN
LOW BACK

REAR VIEW
1) TRAPEZIUS
2) LATISSIMUS

AVOID

LOW BACK
STRAIN
PAIN

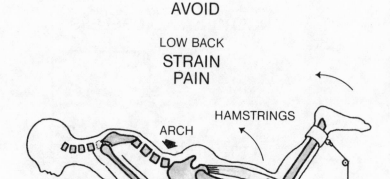

Of all the exercises practiced in weight-lifting gyms, this one is probably the most useless. The only time strengthening the hamstrings is useful is after a knee injury. Otherwise, it's wasted effort. It does, however, pull upon the pelvis, which arches the low back, which leads to trouble.

3. FLEXIBILITY: WHY WE LOSE IT, HOW WE REGAIN IT

The greatest problem associated with aging, the problem that most devastates the body, is not that the bones get softer, as so many people think. It's that the tissues around the bones lose their flexibility. The result:

- We stiffen up and can't move the way we used to.
- It's tougher to raise our arms over our heads.
- When we want to see something to the side or behind us, we can't do it just by turning our heads. We have to turn our bodies.

Stiffness of this sort is only partly due to the passage of time. To a great extent, it is also a consequence of inactivity.

I see patients in their fifties who are as stiff as the proverbial wooden board. I see other patients in their seventies who can do a fair imitation of break dancing. The septuagenarians may have been born with greater flexibility; usually, however, their suppleness is the result of a specific effort to remain flexible.

Before we consider how to regain flexibility, let's determine how and why we lose it.

The Villain: "Adaptive Shortening"

As you sit reading this chapter, a force is at work in your body that can ultimately destroy your flexibility. It's called "adaptive shortening." It occurs because the natural tendency of collagen, the material of which connective tissue is made, is to contract.

Human tissue will never remain elongated on its own; a force must be applied. Given the slightest encouragement, it will retract instead. If you keep your knee bent for any length of time, that knee will remain bent because the tissue behind it will tighten. As your tissues gradually adapt to the bent position, your flexibility diminishes.

Consider now all the ways in which we encourage adaptive shortening in everyday life. Through most of the day we sit with knees and hips flexed, if not at our desks, then in automobiles, buses, trains, and planes, or at the dinner table, or in front of our television sets. Given the nature of our lives, it is all but impossible for anyone to escape the consequences of adaptive shortening.

Try this little test. Seat yourself on the floor with your back against a wall. Now stretch one leg out in front of you. Draw the foot of the other leg up against your thigh. Is the back of the knee of the extended leg flat against the floor? If not, your tissues have contracted. You are no longer as flexible as you once were.

Adaptive shortening is most clearly illustrated by the loss of flexibility in the legs, which remain in a bent position so much of every day. But the rest of the body is equally vulnerable to the constriction of tissue when no force is applied to make the tissue stretch. When this sort of adaptive shortening occurs, we have lost "range of motion."

Here are a few simple tests you can do in front of a mirror to evaluate your range of motion:

Raise your arms over your head until your fingertips point to the ceiling. Notice the position of your arms. Are they in front of your ears, even with your ears, or behind your ears? If you have good range of motion, your arms will be even with your ears or behind them. Are both arms equally mobile? If one is farther back than the other, your range of motion in that arm and shoulder is superior to that of the other arm and shoulder.

Standing sideways to the mirror, put your arms behind you and link your hands together. Now pull your hands away from your back. Good range of motion will enable you to separate your hands from your back by ten to eighteen inches, depending on your height, and to raise the hands to a level even with your waist.

Finally, facing the mirror once again, place your arms at your sides, and without moving your elbows away from your body, turn your hands outward. If you have good range of motion, the palms of each hand will be completely visible. If one palm is more visible than the other, the range of motion is diminished in the arm of the less visible hand.

Flexibility in Close-up

The loss of flexibility can be attributed in large part to the same problem associated with the abuse of the body through overly strenuous exercise—the loss of moisture in our tissue. This concept is so important to an understanding of how and why we age —and how the aging process can be reversed—that it bears review.

Human tissue, as we've noted, acts like a sponge, and like a sponge it can be kept soft or hard depending on how it's used. If you immerse a sponge in water and squeeze the liquid from it, it will suck water back in as soon as you release it. The hydration and nutrition of tissue occurs in exactly the same manner, through compression and relaxation.

It's movement that causes compression and relaxation. When the tissue isn't moved, it simply dries out—just like a sponge that isn't used. The unused sponge shrivels. So does the tissue. Some movement is better than no movement at all, but walking from the bedroom to the kitchen or from the parking lot to your office doesn't provide your tissue with sufficient stimulation to keep it from drying up and aging long before its time.

The process I've just described happens throughout your body —in the cartilage of the joints, in the ligaments that hold the bones together, and in the muscles that move the bones.

Inactivity is only one of the culprits. Emotional stress is another. It, too, can produce changes in tissue and muscle fiber that can profoundly affect flexibility. If you take a careful look at someone you think of as a tense person, you can see what emotional stress has done.

Tense people look tight in their bodies. Their shoulders are hunched over. Their arms are together, their chests drawn in. They are literally curled up, almost in a fetal position.

Emotional tension doesn't exist without physical tension. Whenever there is sustained physical tension, there is adaptive shortening of connective tissue.

If you are a habitually tense person, your muscles are in an almost constant state of contraction, ready for action, tensed for "fight or flight." In this state, the muscles' demand for nourishment is accelerated and the supply of blood in them is soon depleted. Unfortunately, the tissue doesn't relax sufficiently to allow new supplies of blood to enter at a sufficient rate. As a result, both the muscles and the skin that houses them shorten and become less elastic. There then ensues a classic catch-22 situation: What began as emotional tension now becomes physical tension. The increased physical tension—a constant in shortened tissue and muscle—then intensifies your psychological tension. As the cycle continues, you get stiffer and stiffer.

Flexibility is determined by the elasticity of tissue. The elasticity of tissue depends, in turn, on the ability of collagen fibers— the flexible material in tissue—to expand. Both inactivity and tension work against that ability.

If you look at a microscopic sample of tissue, you'll see that the collagen fibers are arranged in a gridlike pattern. When these fibers move, they glide in and out of each other. It is this gliding movement that enables our muscles to lengthen and shorten. As we contract our muscles, the fibers become short. As they stretch,

EXERCISE PREVENTS FIBERS "STICKING"

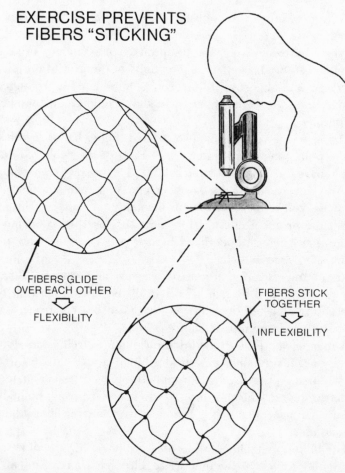

FIBERS GLIDE
OVER EACH OTHER
⇩
FLEXIBILITY

FIBERS STICK
TOGETHER
⇩
INFLEXIBILITY

Collagen fibers, under a microscope, appear as a grid. Ideally, the fibers remain independent, gliding on one another, which enables them to expand and contract in an unimpeded manner. But inactivity causes them to stick together at the points where they intersect. Result: loss of flexibility.

they become longer. As we relax, they glide further and further apart.

When these fibers remain in a contracted or extended position, they tend to bind together at the points of the grid where they intersect. It is almost as if they were soldered. With prolonged contact the intersecting fibers actually become glued together chemically.

Suppose you were to glue two crossed rubber bands together at the point where they intersected. Each of the rubber bands would have lost half of its stretchability. That's exactly what happens to collagen fibers that have become stuck together. Once it happens, you've lost half of your flexibility.

But the problem doesn't stop there. It's not just connective tissue that's being undermined by inactivity. Your muscles are being sabotaged as well.

Recall, once again, that muscles are very much like hot dogs. They're contained by skin. The skin of the muscle is made of elastin and collagen tissue. When that skin shortens because it isn't stretched, the muscle shortens, too.

A muscle that is shortened doesn't pump as well as an elongated one. It's pumping that brings blood to the muscles, so a muscle that's pumping less strongly doesn't get as adequate a supply of blood, which means it doesn't receive proper nourishment. As a consequence, it ages prematurely, and the fibers of the muscle die.

The billion tissue fibers with which we begin life are all we're ever going to get. By the time we're thirty-five we're losing millions of them each year. It's this attrition of the fibers that begins to limit our strength, agility, and flexibility.

If we do nothing, the problem accelerates. We lose more and more fibers. We become less and less strong and agile.

If we act intelligently, however, we can not only slow the aging process for a spell but actually reverse it.

The Magic of Proper Movement

The problem with all the changes taking place in our tissue is that we aren't aware of them until we suddenly discover we can't move our bodies in the manner we once could. By that time, some loss of flexibility has already occurred.

Once tissue has become totally dehydrated or the fibers are soldered together, the condition is irreversible. But any time short of that, miracles can happen. The tissue can be rejuvenated by movement specifically designed to make it compress and relax, compress and relax. Fluid will once again reappear in the tissue, and you'll soon be able to throw your arms over your head as you did when you were younger, or look behind you without having to turn your entire body.

You've got to move to animate your tissue. It's movement that makes tissue work like a sponge, keeping it soft and moist. It's movement that dissolves the connections between fibers, allowing them once again to extend to their full capacity. It's movement that can rejuvenate your tissues.

Any movement helps, provided it isn't violent, but to really do the job right you have to stretch in a systematic manner. Proper stretching does it all—nourishing tissue, lubricating joints, contracting and nourishing muscles.

Restoring or improving flexibility is the first, most important step in a rejuvenation program. Without an improvement in flexibility, no other changes are possible. We begin by reawakening lethargic, all but dead, tissue. We energize and liquify it. We gently free up the body's fibers.

To be flexible, you need to stretch every part of your body in a proper manner every single day. You'll learn exactly how to do that in Part Two. For now, take a minute to stand up and stretch. And while you're up, check out your posture in a mirror. Are you "standing tall"? If not, you're aging yourself in ways you never suspected.

4. STANDING TALL: MORE THAN JUST COSMETICS

Whenever I talk about posture, someone is sure to remark that we humans were never meant to walk in an upright position. It's the weight placed on our spines when we reared up on our hind legs that produced our deteriorated disks, as well as our rounded shoulders and pot bellies—or so the speaker asserts.

There are two problems with this argument. First, it ignores our long history as two-legged animals. And second, it ignores evidence that many four-legged animals are even more prone to disk disease than humans.

It's conjecture that we were never made to be two-legged animals. It's fact that we've been two-legged animals since mankind's time on earth began. Even though we might not have evolved from two-legged animals, we *are* two-legged animals. Our task is to make the best of that reality.

Few of us manage to do that, particularly after thirty-five.

The antecedents of poor posture go all the way back to childhood. How we carry ourselves then determines our bearing as we age. But the problems aren't that apparent when we're younger. Throughout our school days, most of us remain physically active, and that activity may carry over well into our twenties and early thirties. But gradually the emphasis changes as we develop new interests. We immerse ourselves in occupations and professions and take up more sedentary hobbies. Before long, there's little time for the physical activity that was once a part of every day. By the time we reach our late thirties, the physical consequences are

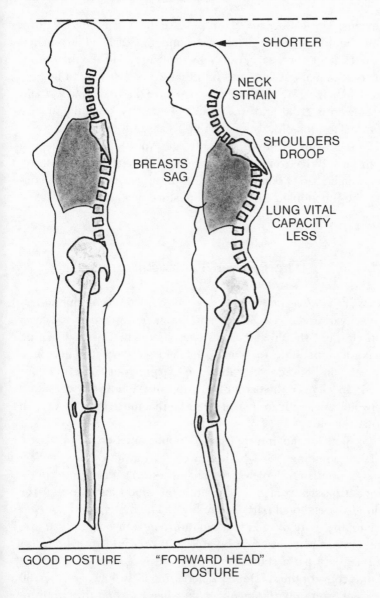

GOOD POSTURE   "FORWARD HEAD" POSTURE

The price of faulty posture: loss of height, drooping shoulders, strain on the spine, loss of vital capacity, and sagging chest.

obvious. There's a curve to our posture that wasn't there before. Our shoulders, once square, are rounded. Our head has inched forward. Our chest sags, our belly protrudes. We see the doctor for our annual checkup and find that we've lost half an inch or more in height. We no longer seem to have the vital capacity to do what we once did and would still like to do. Not only are we starting to look old, we're starting to act old, too.

Poor posture is unattractive. It ages you more than lines in your face. If that were the only problem associated with posture, it would be bad enough. It's not. Far more serious than cosmetics are the functional problems bad posture produces.

The Price of Faulty Posture

A loss of vital capacity. Poor posture depletes your pulmonary capacity by as much as 30 percent. Permanently constricted chest muscles and shoulder muscles overly stretched from drooping make it impossible for you to expand your chest. There is a correlation between your ability to expand your chest and your vital capacity. To the extent that you can expand your chest and fill your lungs with air, you are putting that much more oxygen in your system.

Oxygen has an indispensable double function in our lives. First, it combines with the food we eat to produce energy. Second, it nourishes depleted tissue and restores it to prime condition. It passes from the lungs into the blood and through the blood vessels to all parts of the body. The better condition you are in, the more oxygen you can utilize in your body. But to use the oxygen you must first be able to take it into your body.

Imagine what a shot of energy you'd give your body on the tennis court or the ski slope by increasing its supply of oxygen 30 percent. You only think you're old when exertion tires you unduly, when in fact you've lost endurance simply because your posture won't let you breathe as well as you once could.

You can get an idea of your vital capacity by measuring your chest expansion, as follows:

- Place a soft tape measure around your chest, across your shoulder blades in back and at the level of your breastbone in front.
- Measure your chest with the air expelled from your lungs.
- Take a deep breath, as deep as possible.
- Measure your chest again.

The difference between the first measurement and the second is your chest expansion.

Smaller people will have a smaller chest expansion than larger people. Generally speaking, however, your expanded chest should be 8 to 10 percent larger than your chest with the air expelled from your lungs. If it's less than that, it means in all probability that your vital capacity is not what it ought to be.

A few simple exercises—which we'll demonstrate in Part Two —will increase the expansion of your rib cage by one half to three quarters of an inch within a month's time, and improve your vital capacity by 10 to 15 percent.

A loss of proper function. Rounding out affects your entire gastro-intestinal system, particularly your bowels. "I can't move my damn bowels" is probably the most frequent complaint physicians hear from patients past thirty-five.

Your intestines are connected to your spine by a string of tissue. If your spine is fairly straight, the string holds your bowel taut, the position in which it functions best. If your spine arches and sways forward, your intestines sag and come to rest on your pelvic floor. The effect is something like a garden hose that has been snagged and bent instead of neatly coiled. The passage of matter is inhibited.

A loss of range of motion. As your skeleton changes—as a slumped-over position becomes more and more the norm—your tissues must also adapt. We've seen that the muscles and ligaments that make your skeleton mobile are like rubber bands, and that, like rubber bands, they shorten if they don't get pulled. Once your tissues have adapted to a shortened state, they will no longer stretch to the degree they once did. Trying to stretch them as before will be difficult, painful and—if you've permitted the condition to solidify—all but impossible.

Just as poor posture permanently shortens certain muscles, it permanently stretches others. If your shoulders are forward and down most of the time, the muscles in the shoulders and between the shoulder blades have been stretched and overstretched to the point of losing their ability to retract to their normal length.

Muscles and ligaments that have been shortened or stretched no longer function as they should. In this manner, poor posture has reduced your body's range of motion.

There are other consequences to poor posture that further impede range of motion.

When you're hunched over, you have placed a mechanical limitation on the motion of your neck. When you try to turn your head, you can't do it without also turning your torso. That's a serious loss of function. Consider how important it is to be able to look quickly and painlessly to your left or right when you're driving a car or attempting to cross a street. Yes, you can still see the car in the lane beside you, and you can still check the cars approaching the intersection, but not as quickly or efficiently, and not without discomfort.

When you're round-shouldered, you can't fully raise your arms. It's a mechanical impossibility. Your shoulder blades get in

Range of motion in the shoulders depends in great part on good erect posture. When you're slumped over, your arms won't go overhead; they're mechanically blocked by the shoulder blades. Good posture removes that impediment.

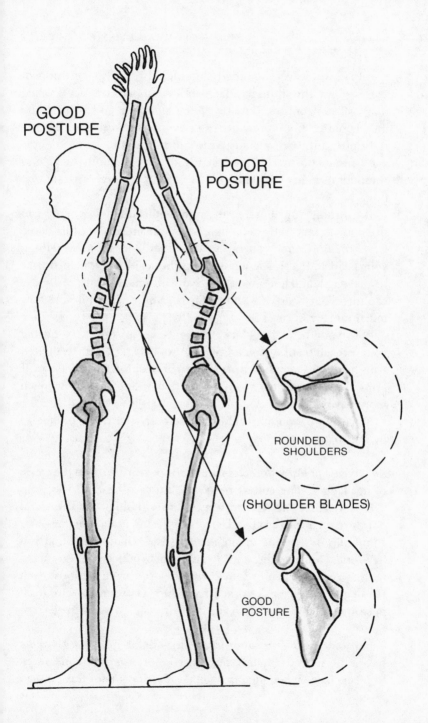

GOOD
POSTURE

POOR
POSTURE

ROUNDED
SHOULDERS

(SHOULDER BLADES)

GOOD
POSTURE

the way. Worse yet, rounded shoulders produce a collision of bones where the shoulder blade and the upper arm meet. When that collision occurs, bursitis of the shoulder and pain in the muscle of the shoulder blade result. If your shoulders were in the right position, such a collision would not occur.

A simple postural adjustment can increase both head and shoulder mobility by 50 percent or more. Let's demonstrate that now.

Try turning your head to the right and to the left when it's in the same position it's been in as you've been reading this book. Carefully note what you can see to either side. Next, straighten your head so that it's in a good upright position. Now turn your head to right and left once again. Note how much more easily you can turn your head, how much farther you can turn it, and how much more you can see.

With your head in a forward, bent-over posture, try raising your arms in front of you as high as they will go. Next, straighten your head once again to a good upright position. Now raise your arms again. Note how much higher they will go, and how much more easily they move.

In Part Two, you'll learn how to increase your range of motion by improving your posture.

An increase in discomfort and pain. Poor posture is often the cause of headaches. The culprit here is a "forward head."

It's extremely difficult to work in a technological society and not develop a forward head. If you're sitting at a typewriter or a computer, or working on an assembly line, chances are that you have one. Even cooking and cleaning can produce one. Any activity that requires you to look down for protracted periods, even reading or simple desk work, can produce a chronic forward head position. Such a posture can, in turn, lead to pain in the jaw joints.

Jaw joint pain is so widespread today that a majority of adults have experienced it. This type of discomfort was once considered to be exclusively a dental problem, caused by malocclusion, bad

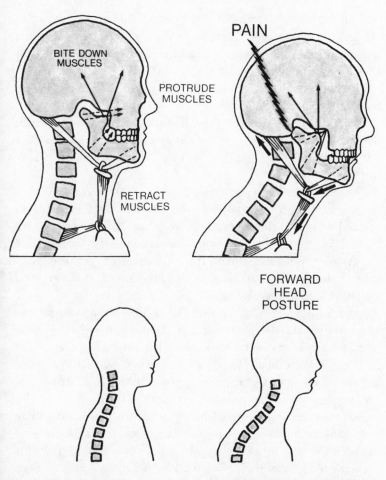

PAIN

BITE DOWN
MUSCLES

PROTRUDE
MUSCLES

RETRACT
MUSCLES

FORWARD
HEAD
POSTURE

Forward head posture produces "TMJ," temporomandibular joint
disease. The symptoms: an abnormal bite, pain and grinding of
the jaw joint.

teeth, or irregular jaw formation. While these problems can still
produce the pain, we now know that it is just as often caused or
aggravated by faulty posture.

Rounded shoulders can also produce their share of pain. They pull on the trapezius muscles that connect the outer extremity of the shoulder blade and the base of the skull. The strain of that pull produces the headaches you often feel at the base of your skull where the shoulder muscles attach.

The final problem produced by poor posture is the most common one of all: low backache.

Those of us who are over thirty-five are probably more anxious about our lower backs—the lumbar spine area—than any other part of our body. It's the part that most frequently reminds us of our age.

The lumbar spine is constructed of five vertebrae that stretch from just above the tailbone to the rib cage. Like little blocks stacked one upon the other, these vertebrae balance on the tailbone. It is where the tailbone and the vertebrae join that we have the greatest spinal movement. It is also where we have the greatest spinal angle. Not surprisingly, this junction offers the greatest potential for back problems.

At its lower extremity, the spine takes off from the sacrum, the bone that forms the posterior wall of the pelvis. Because the sacrum itself is angled rather than vertical, the spine takes off at an angle. It must then curve back again to get back to its center of gravity. The crucial factor is how great a curve it must make. The greater the curve, the greater the potential for problems.

Excessive curving stretches muscles and tissues, making them vulnerable to injury. Excessive curving also narrows the distance between the vertebrae on the inside of the curve, which not only presses on the disks but impinges on the nerves that pass through the windows of the spine to other parts of the body. Results: irritation, aches, and spasms.

Are you a candidate for low back pain? One simple test is to compare your height today with what it was ten or twenty years ago. If you're more than half an inch shorter, it almost certainly means that your spine is more curved today than it was in that earlier period. The greater the curve, the greater the likelihood that you will experience low back pain.

Further on, we'll be working on exercises to arrest and even

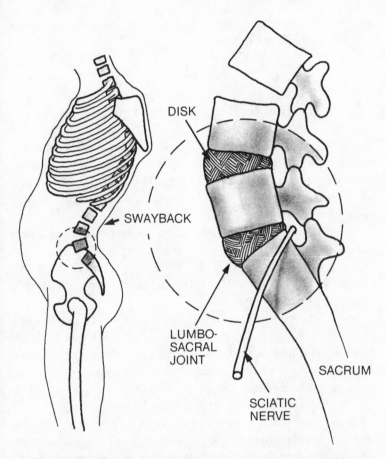

DISK

SWAYBACK

LUMBO-
SACRAL
JOINT

SACRUM

SCIATIC
NERVE

Low backache is the most common problem associated with aging, and poor posture is its most common cause. The poorer your posture, the greater the curve, or lordosis, in your low back. The greater the lordosis, the greater the chance for pain due to excessive stretching of tissue and pressure on disks and nerves.

reverse the shrinking process—the best possible insurance against low back pain.

How to Regain Good Posture

Your body has a center of gravity. All of your body's segments must line up along that center of gravity. Your center of gravity transects four curves in your body. The more shallow those curves, the closer they come to your center of gravity and the more efficient you are.

An "efficient" posture is one that's perfectly balanced with a minimum amount of energy, and produces no pain. It makes you look and feel young and vital. An "inefficient" posture is one that somehow breaches the relationship of your body parts with your center of gravity.

Your body must stay in balance; one curve must compensate for another. If you develop a marked sway of your low back, for example, you must also develop a sway of your upper back and neck. These curves work to balance you around the one constant in your posture—your center of gravity. The greater those curves, the less efficient your body's engineering.

Chances are that you won't be aware of how inefficient you've become, or even aware of the changes in your body's alignment. Your curves developed and your tissues adapted so gradually over the years that your posture now seems perfectly normal. Let's find out if it is.

- Stand against a wall.
- Place your heels six inches away from the baseboard and push your low back flat against the wall, until you feel it touching.
- Now check the distance between your head and the wall and your neck and the wall by feeling with your fingers. If your posture is good, your head and most of your neck will be no more than three fingers' width from the wall.

Next, stand with your head touching the wall and your heels once again six inches from the baseboard.

• With your buttocks touching the wall, check the distance between your lower back and the wall, and your neck and the wall.

• If you can get within an inch or two at the low back and two inches at the neck, you are close to having excellent posture.

Small deviations from these ideal positions are normal. You need have little concern about your posture if your deviations from these ideal positions are minor. Larger deviations mean that you are among those whose postural problems are restricting their activities and limiting their lives.

Good posture, like good engineering, contributes to good function. Regaining good posture should be a primary objective of anyone who wants to reverse the effects of aging—functionally as well as cosmetically.

For many of you over thirty-five, this admonition will produce an automatic response. You'll tuck your buttocks, square your shoulders, and suck in your stomach, just as generations of physical education instructors have admonished us to do. It's a fine idea, but it doesn't work.

Good posture does mandate a decrease in the angle of the pelvis and the curve in our lower spine, and those recommended movements accomplish just that. The problem is that the position is a difficult one to maintain. First, it's muscularly impractical, and second, we must keep reminding ourselves to maintain it. No matter how hard we try to think about it, in a few moments we forget.

There is a more basic problem still. The old method neglects the most important body component of all where posture is concerned: the head.

The objective of good posture is to achieve the most efficient possible alignment of your body segments. This means straightening out those curves in your spine, bringing them as close to

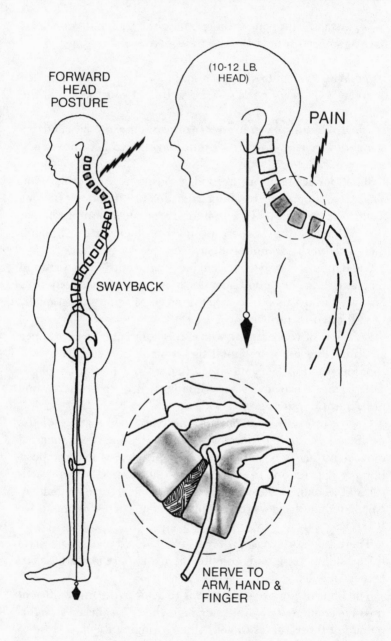

FORWARD
HEAD
POSTURE

SWAYBACK

(10-12 LB.
HEAD)

PAIN

NERVE TO
ARM, HAND &
FINGER

your center of gravity as you possibly can. There is one simple, infallible way to do it, and that is to raise your head.

As we age, the head begins to slump forward, almost imperceptibly at first, more noticeably later on. As this occurs, it changes the entire balance of the body. The head weighs anywhere from ten to fifteen pounds. If the body did nothing to compensate for the forward thrust of the head, it would be unbalanced, making standing and walking extremely difficult. So the body compensates for the change by altering the center of gravity. It does so by deepening the curves in the spine.

There are four such curves, beginning in the neck and ending at the sacrum. There is one and only one way to straighten all four curves at once, and that is by adjusting the position of the head.

This point is so important that I would like you to prove it to yourself. You'll need a large mirror and a small one that you can hold in your hand.

- Place yourself in front of the large mirror.
- Turn ninety degrees in either direction, so that you're standing sideways to the mirror.
- Hold the small mirror in such a fashion that you can see your figure in the large mirror.
- Carefully observe your posture, making certain that it's your normal posture and that you haven't made any adjustments.
- Now, pull your head back and raise it toward the ceiling.

Unless you are ramrod straight to begin with, there is no way you won't observe a significant change.

Here's what it looks like when your head begins to droop. A forward head puts extra weight on the joints at the back of the neck. That closes the windows of the spine, pinching the nerves.

What you have done with that *single* adjustment is to put your entire body into its proper alignment.

Standing Tall

Several years ago, a South African radiologist investigated a group of hemp workers, all of whom had marked swaybacks. A swayback is an excessive or abnormal curvature of the spinal column in the lumbar region. It usually produces backaches. But these workers didn't have backaches, even though their work required them to carry fifty-pound bundles of hemp on their heads, an exercise that would seem likely to exacerbate the problem. The radiologist determined to find out why.

First, he took X rays of the workers in a normal standing posture. The X rays showed exactly what he had thought they would; the workers all had tilted tailbones that caused their backs to sway. For his next set of X rays, the radiologist had the workers balance a fifty-pound weight on their heads. The change in the spinal configuration was astonishing. With the weights on their heads, the workers' tailbones were anywhere from 20 to 40 percent more upright, and the change manifested itself all the way through the spinal column.

When you put a weight on your head, you have to make a physical effort to support it. As you make this effort, you automatically adjust your body segments along your center of gravity. This adjustment keeps the weight from becoming too heavy.

To adjust, you must push up. As you push up, you decrease your spinal curves—the sway of your back, neck, and chest.

Let's demonstrate with a simple experiment. If you put a five-pound weight on your head, and you do nothing more than push up against the resistance, you will straighten out your spinal curves without so much as a thought. It is the weight that's doing the work by giving your body feedback, telling it to push up toward the ceiling, and to stand tall. To your body, any other response is intolerable. If your head were to move forward, back, or to either side, the weight would become heavier in proportion to the amount you tilt. At a one-inch tilt, the weight would increase to ten pounds; at two inches, fifteen pounds; at three inches, twenty pounds. It would become such a strain on your neck muscles that you would automatically correct and start to push back, straightening your entire body in the process.

The most important step you can take to improve your posture is to gain a sense of what good posture feels like in your own body. In Part Two, we'll be doing a series of exercises to restore your posture or put you in the proper alignment for the first time in your life. For now, think about standing tall. Each time you think about it, push your head to the ceiling. You'll quickly sense the difference—and see it, as well.

A Special Note for Women

During the course of my research for this book, I traveled to Hawaii to give a series of lectures. On the beach one morning, I spent an hour observing the postures of the people parading by. I saw hundreds of examples of what I've just described: forward heads, rounded shoulders, sagging chests, protruding bellies. And I noted something among the women—an absolute correlation between the position of their shoulders and the position of their breasts. The more rounded their shoulders, the more their breasts sagged.

Aging produces a normal amount of sagging of the breasts. The muscle, fat, and skin in and around the breasts lose a certain amount of tone over the years. But this natural attrition is responsible for only half of the loss of a youthful bustline. The other half is a consequence of a rounding of the shoulders—in other words, poor posture.

Improvement of the bustline through improved posture is a basic part of the training of women who want to be models.

Models need to project an image of youth and vitality, whereas sagging breasts and rounded backs project an image of age.

Any woman, no matter what her age, can reduce the sag in her breasts by 50 percent simply by standing tall.

The Rejuvenation Strategy: Summing Up

The magic word is "tissue." Neglected, it shrivels and dries, and makes you stiff and prematurely old in the process. Exercised regularly and properly, it springs back to life, restoring that youthful suppleness you imagined was gone forever.

One simple postural adjustment—"standing tall"—can make you look years younger and restore vital function and mobility to your body.

No arduous workouts are required. To the contrary, as we're about to see, many of the movements are so simple that they can be incorporated into daily activities.

On to the program.

PART TWO

THE REJUVENATION PROGRAM

5. FIVE SHORT STEPS TO A YOUTHFUL LIFE

The two major problems of aging, flexibility and posture, can be corrected with a single set of exercises. When you exercise to improve your posture, you're automatically increasing your flexibility.

The five easy steps in this program move from the top to the bottom of your body. In the process, they deal with every problem area associated with aging, addressing problems you may have developed already, and preparing defenses against new ones.

You'll find no gimmicks here, but rather a series of tissue-rejuvenating movements that have met the test of time. Taking these five easy steps will make you feel and look younger in a matter of weeks.

Each step is vital. While all are related, the individual steps make distinct contributions to your conditioning. Stretching, for example, elongates your muscles, but it doesn't make them strong. You need special exercises to do that. And neither stretching nor strengthening exercises do anything for cardiovascular conditioning, an important component of your program.

Many men and women who haven't exercised since childhood wonder whether it's safe for them to undertake an exercise program when they're middle-aged or older, and they worry the most about cardiovascular conditioning. The concern is a logical one, but it's misplaced. As indicated earlier, experience has taught us that inactivity is far more threatening than exercise.

If exercise is done sensibly, progressively, and slowly, it can't be anything but beneficial. If you strain too hard when you exercise, it can raise your blood pressure temporarily and detrimentally. But exercise in moderation will so improve your overall condition that your normal blood pressure will drop. And an improvement in posture and flexibility will do wonders for your gastrointestinal system.

The only people who should be concerned about exercising are those with joint damage, heart disease, or other disease patterns suggesting the possibility of a stroke. In any case, such people should be under the care of a physician.

Before embarking on any exercise program, this one included, it is your responsibility to discuss it with your physician. If he has you on a special program because of your health, he and you will want to evaluate carefully which part of the Rejuvenation Program you can follow, and which you should avoid. If your condition is good, your physician will undoubtedly urge you to proceed. Should he tell you to "take it easy," it's up to you to ask him, "What does that mean?" In the unlikely event that your physician tells you not to exercise at all even though your health is good, you ought to ask, "Why?"

As a final measure of reassurance, you should bear in mind that most of the exercises you'll be doing are so simple and undemanding they might better be called rejuvenation "movements." They certainly don't deserve the sense of sweat and strain the word "exercise" conveys.

The word is misleading in yet another way. We think of exercise as something quite formal done within a time frame. But you can't exercise twenty minutes a day to improve your posture, and then disregard your posture for the other waking hours. Posture is something you must practice at all times, not simply when you're standing or walking but when you're seated as well. Sitting in a bad posture is detrimental because it ages the tissues. As we've seen, the reason most of us age prematurely is that we remain in one position throughout the day, thereby permanently shortening muscles and drying out tissue.

Basically, there are three categories of exercisers. There are those who have exercised most of their lives. Many of them are athletically endowed and devoted to their sport and whatever it takes to keep them fit to practice it. Then there are those who, owing to an illness or an impairment, have lost some degree of function and are exercising to regain it. Finally, there is the third group, by far the largest, consisting of people who would like to achieve an acceptable level of fitness but don't want to distort their lives in the process.

The third group is generally deconditioned, people who are so busy with their careers that they haven't paid attention to their bodies. One day they look in the mirror and don't like what it tells them. They can see that they're overweight; looking a little more closely, they can also see that they're sagging, head and shoulders forward, stomach protruding. They can do wonders to that image simply by straightening up. All the joints move; all at once they'll look thinner and taller. Most of the gut will disappear. Would that they could or would stay that way after turning from the mirror. It doesn't happen. A minute later, they'll be back in their slouch.

It doesn't work to be given a concept of posture without appropriate physiological preparation to accompany it. People who have neglected themselves must undergo a specific program until they are back to an appropriate maintenance level.

So while our eventual objective is to incorporate most of the exercises that follow into daily life, let's begin with a little structure.

An Everyday Affair

Most exercise physiologists and specialists in sports medicine agree that you should always rest your body for a day after a bout of strenuous, violent exercise. Basically, that's good advice. But our exercise regime is neither strenuous nor violent and ought to be done every day.

In strenuous forms of exercise, you're causing the muscles to contract. In the process, the muscles use up oxygen, and accumulate toxins. They need a day off to get rid of the toxins and recuperate from the strain.

Our exercise performs a totally different function. Where violent exercise contracts the muscles, all the movements in our regime—except those in Chapter 9, which are designed specifically for strength—simply stretch the muscles. There is no trauma, and no buildup of toxins.

Stretching every day is the only way we can maintain a maximum amount of flexibility. Remember the rubber band that doesn't get stretched. It dries and shortens—and breaks when you finally do get around to stretching it. The same goes for the body's tissue.

Nothing is more important to the maintenance of a youthful body than a daily bout of stretching in a manner designed with the body's traditional trouble spots in mind. Every other day won't do. The older you are, the more important it becomes. You can exercise three days a week and stay reasonably fit, but you can be more fit by exercising five, six, or seven days a week. Fitness is a daily process.

If you play a sport or lift weights, it's wise to take a day off in between those events. But even on the off days, you should have some degree of physical activity in order to maintain flexibility as well as cardiovascular stimulation. Either you're using an entirely different set of muscles for an entirely different purpose, or else you're using the same muscles in an entirely different way.

Warming Up

Whenever you're about to move your body in any manner more strenuous than walking, it would be wise to recall those gridlike images made by the collagen in your tissue. "Solder points," we called them, the infinitesimal junctions of the fibers. When you've been inactive for a number of hours, particularly after a long sleep, your body feels stiff when you begin to move. That's because the crisscrossing fibers are adhering to one another at the junction points. Getting them free of one another requires some body heat. It's a delicate operation at the outset, because any abrupt or violent movement could cause the tissue to tear.

How do you heat the body? It's warm blood that does it, blood that circulates in the vessels and moves to the extremities. A hot bath or shower will get the blood moving after it has cooled down overnight. I treat patients who are so stiff and sore on arising that they can scarcely move. For them to exercise in such condition would all but guarantee problems; in such cases a hot bath or shower first is mandatory. If that's the condition you find yourself in each morning, then you should follow suit. But if you experience only a normal amount of stiffness when you get out of bed, there are less time-consuming methods for dealing with it.

Most fitness coaches counsel a ten- to fifteen-minute warm-up before a bout of exercise. That's probably a good idea if you're about to undertake an extreme form of exercise, but it's difficult to justify in our case. First, the exercises you're about to do are not extreme; second, they are designed to be done regularly during a compact period of time. No exercise program is any good if it isn't followed on a regular basis, and most people don't have the luxury of fifteen minutes to warm up before getting to the exercises themselves.

Nonetheless, getting the blood to surge through the body is a good idea before stretching, so what we need is a method that will accomplish that quickly and avoid pounding the cartilage in the joints as conventional warm-up movements—jogging, running in place, jumping jacks—do.

The solution: Isometric Tension.

As you lie in bed just after awakening, tighten the muscles of your entire body with all the strength you have. Hold for a count of five. Then relax. Repeat that same sequence five to ten times and you have surged the blood through your muscles without putting any stress on your joints.

The above assumes that you're going to be exercising immediately upon arising. All things considered, it's probably the best time. Your body is stiffer than it will be in the afternoon and evening, but it's a good way to loosen yourself up for the day ahead—and if you do it then, you've got it behind you. Otherwise, you can easily let the day slip by without doing your exercises.

But the Isometric Tension routine is good any time of the day. Just lie down on the floor before you exercise and go through the same clenching-relaxing routine.

For good measure, I recommend that you add either the supine bicycle exercise or the swinging warm-up shown on pages 75 and 76. Doing both would be ideal.

"Train, Don't Strain"

The best advice ever invented for those who seek to improve their performance or physical condition is "Train, don't strain." Improvement happens so swiftly once you've committed yourself to daily workouts that there is no need to push it. This is especially true for those who haven't exercised in years; their improvement, relative to their condition, will be the most dramatic of all—and without exerting as much effort as the person who either is in better shape to begin with, or is years younger. Benefits are as relative to age as they are to physical condition; at thirty-five you'll be able to stretch more than at sixty-two, but your muscles at sixty-two will get a greater relative benefit from less stretching.

Stretching should be approached conservatively at any age. In addition to learning what not to do, you'll want to remember *how* not to do it. In two words: *Don't bounce.*

What you're stretching is the capsular tissue of muscle—the skin of the hot dog; anatomically the fibers of tissue have been shown to do much better when they are stretched in a sustained manner. The objective is to get the nerve controls of the muscles to relax electrically and chemically. Slow and sustained elongation does that. Bouncing, on the other hand, triggers a reflex mechanism that causes the muscles to contract—exactly the opposite of what you're trying to achieve.

When you're exercising, be your own physician.

BEDROOM BICYCLING

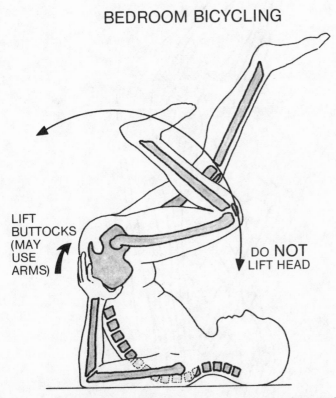

LIFT BUTTOCKS (MAY USE ARMS)

DO **NOT** LIFT HEAD

This supine bicycle exercise helps you in a variety of ways. First, it's a good warm-up for any bout of exercise. Second, it gently stretches the low back. Third, it strengthens abdominal and leg muscles. Fourth, it provides cardiovascular stimulation. Do twenty-five repetitions at first, and work up to fifty. Remember: This is a warm-up exercise. Move slowly and gently.

SWINGING WARMUP

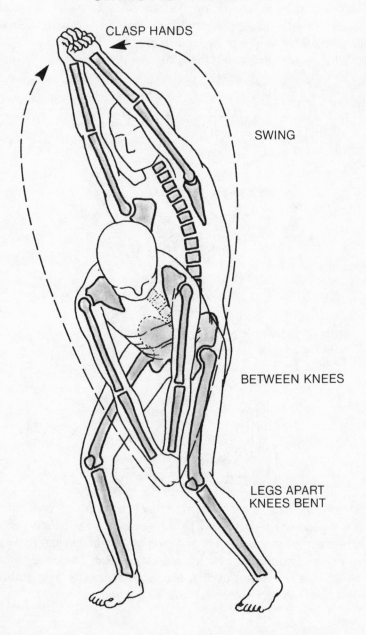

CLASP HANDS

SWING

BETWEEN KNEES

LEGS APART
KNEES BENT

Pain is an indication that something is being moved or abused in a manner that it shouldn't be. The athlete works out to that point because it gives him a signal that he has strained to his maximum. When the time comes for him to extend himself to gain first place instead of second or third, he'll be familiar with the feeling of pain, as well as with the sensations of straining to that point.

If there is a momentary sense of discomfort associated with a movement, but no residual pain once the movement is stopped, you're not really hurting yourself. But any lasting pain means that a special substance called prostaglandin has been secreted into your soft tissue, irritating the nerves and producing the sensation you're feeling. The young athlete may need to accustom himself to such sensations; all you're doing after the age of thirty-five is increasing the danger of injury. At that point, you're on the threshold. If you feel any pain as you proceed, do yourself a favor: Pull back.

Let's move now through each step of the Rejuvenation Program. As you read, simply familiarize yourself with the movements, trying each of them in turn. But don't feel that you need to remember each movement. We'll put them all together into a comprehensive program at the end of Part Two.

With your knees flexed and your feet spread, clasp your hands together and swing them over your head and then through your legs, bending at the waist and knees in the process. Move slowly and gently. Repeat fifteen to twenty times without interruption. As your condition improves, you may wish to hold a light weight in your hands, and increase the number of repetitions.

6. STEP ONE:
USING YOUR HEAD

The head is the most neglected body part in fitness programs. It's an integral part of this one.

It's an axiom of sports performance that the body follows the head. If you want to do a front flip, you first tuck your chin; to do a back flip, you tilt the head backward. The axiom applies to posture. You can realign your entire body just by moving your head.

Most people working on their posture worry about the position of their shoulders and pelvis. Both are important to a correct alignment. But as we saw in Chapter 4, the position of the head is more important still. When you push your head back, it automatically decreases your pelvic curve as well as your neck curve. Your chest rises and your shoulders square up.

Working to realign the head is a perfect example of how exercise can be deregimented and incorporated into everyday life. Every time you come to a stoplight while you're driving your car, you can use those seconds of waiting to do several of the simple exercises you'll be doing to help you regain an erect posture.

At the outset, however, you will want to practice the exercises in a more formal way.

If you have not exercised your neck regularly in the past, it is undoubtedly stiff and inflexible. The exercises given below are designed to make the neck limber. At the same time, they will encourage you to avoid a "forward head." Remember that with your head held in a forward position, you can add up to thirty pounds of pull on the cervical spine. That's enough to pull your entire body out of line. We've already added up the cost: loss of vital capacity, increase in pain and discomfort, loss of good bowel function, loss of range of motion.

The following exercises will lower and eliminate that cost. Repeat them whenever possible throughout the day.

Reminders

The key to all the neck exercises is: Chin in, head high.

When you're not exercising, try to get into the habit of pulling back from what you're doing and standing tall. Think of a beanbag on your head and push it toward the ceiling.

The result of all this effort will be to add height you've probably lost, first by decreasing the curves in your spine, second by swelling dried-out disks with fluid. As your condition improves, you'll be able to stand straighter with better support, further augmenting your height. You can't regain all your lost height; there's always some attrition. But if you're an inch shorter than you were ten years ago, you can gain back seven-eighths of that inch by following the exercises in this chapter for two to three months.

One caution: At all times, whether you're exercising or not, avoid tilting the head back unduly. That angle of the head only increases the curvature of the neck. You can also hurt yourself. By tilting the head back, you jam the joints of the spine together, closing all the windows in the back of the neck and greatly increasing the likelihood of pinching the nerves.

HEAD FORWARD AND BACK-HOLD

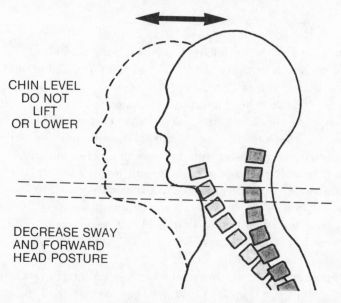

CHIN LEVEL
DO NOT
LIFT
OR LOWER

DECREASE SWAY
AND FORWARD
HEAD POSTURE

This simple exercise improves posture and decreases excessive neck curvature, a condition that can cause neck pain, induce arthritic changes of the neck joints, and produce numbness, tingling sensations, pain, and weakness in the arms, hands, and fingers. Improved head and neck posture will also minimize muscular headaches. The exercise can be done anywhere, at any time and should be done frequently.

Tuck your chin in, then move it forward and back as though you are sliding it along a greasy board, emphasizing the backward more than the forward motion. Do five repetitions. For variation, turn your head to the left or right. Hold the head in the back position after each repetition.

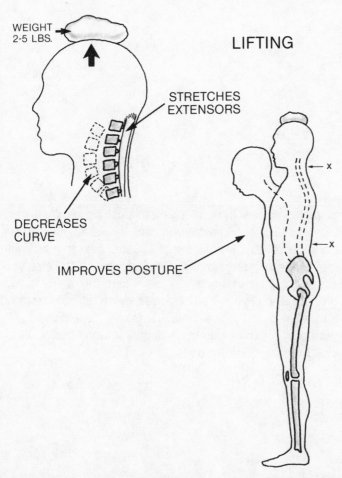

WEIGHT 2-5 LBS.

LIFTING

STRETCHES EXTENSORS

DECREASES CURVE

IMPROVES POSTURE

x

x

This exercise will give you the feeling of "standing tall." **1.** Place a weight of two to five pounds on the top of your head. A bag of sugar, flour, or rice will do fine. **2.** Sit or stand erect with your neck in good alignment, and your chin tucked in. **3.** Try to elongate your neck by pushing your head up into the weight, aiming it at the ceiling. Keep your shoulders down. **4.** Do five repetitions. A light weight on the head will not damage the spinal disks.

This simple exercise will improve general posture, eliminate neck strain, decrease degenerative arthritis of the neck, diminish jaw pains, and decrease low back sway. **1.** Stand next to a wall with your feet a few inches from it. **2.** Flex your knees. **3.** Drive your low back against the wall until you feel it touching. **4.** Then, with your chin level, pull your head back as much as possible, and hold for a slow count of five. Relax. **5.** Do five repetitions.

If your head doesn't touch the wall at first, don't fret. You'll be astounded at how quickly it does.

STANDING TALL

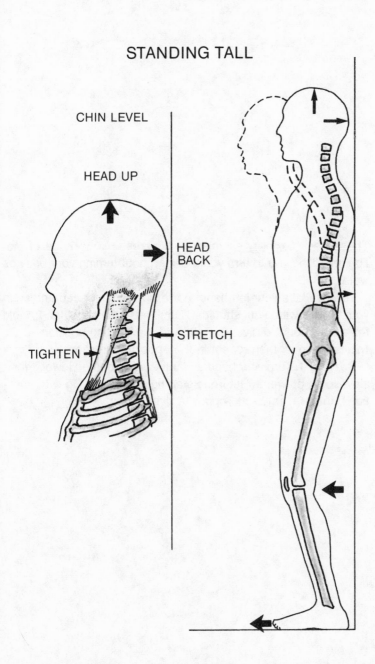

These neck flexibility exercises will increase your range of motion, enabling you to turn your head without turning your body as well.

TOP: 1. Place your left hand at the side of your head and push your head toward your shoulder. Don't raise the shoulder. **2.** Hold for a slow count of five. **3.** Return to the starting position. **4.** Do two repetitions, then repeat in the opposite direction.

BOTTOM: 1. Turn your head as far as it will go, then lower it for a slow count of five. **2.** Return to starting position. **3.** Do two repetitions, then repeat in the opposite direction.

NECK STRETCH

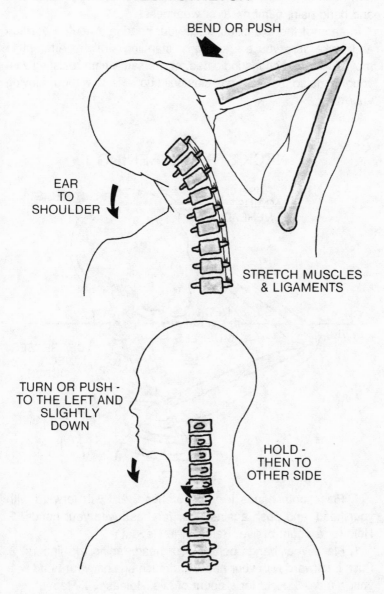

BEND OR PUSH

EAR
TO
SHOULDER

STRETCH MUSCLES
& LIGAMENTS

TURN OR PUSH -
TO THE LEFT AND
SLIGHTLY
DOWN

HOLD -
THEN TO
OTHER SIDE

The next simple exercises will improve posture, decrease excessive neck curvature and degenerative arthritis, and prevent arm and hand pain, numbness, or weakness.

In each of the exercises, keep your head in a neutral position and make sure you are sitting or standing straight. Attempt to move in the directions indicated, at the same time resisting with your hands so that your muscles build up tension without moving your neck.

NECK STRENGTHENING 1

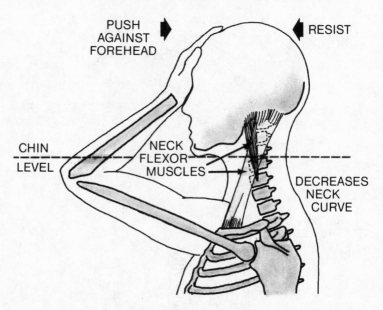

PUSH AGAINST FOREHEAD

RESIST

CHIN LEVEL

NECK FLEXOR MUSCLES

DECREASES NECK CURVE

1. Place both hands to your forehead. **2.** Push forward with your head, and push against your forehead with your hands. **3.** Hold for a count of five. Release. **4.** Repeat.

1. Place your hands behind your head, lacing the fingers. **2.** Push backward with your head, and push against your head with your hands. **3.** Hold for a count of five. Release. **4.** Repeat.

NECK STRENGTHENING 2

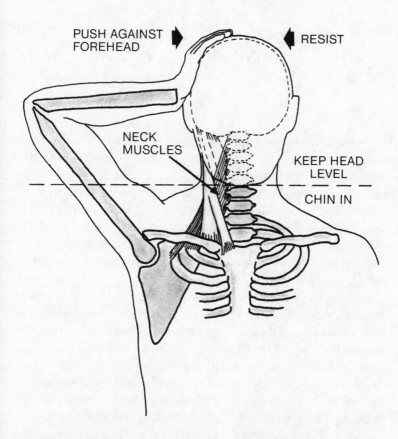

PUSH AGAINST FOREHEAD

RESIST

NECK MUSCLES

KEEP HEAD LEVEL

CHIN IN

This exercise will strengthen neck muscles, flexors, and extensors; improve posture; and minimize damage in case of injury. **1.** Place your right hand on the right side of your forehead. **2.** Attempt to turn your head to the right. Resist with pressure from your hand. **3.** Hold for a count of five. Release. **4.** Do two repetitions. **5.** Then place your left hand on the left side of your forehead and repeat the exercise.

7. STEP TWO: EXTENDING YOUR RANGE OF MOTION

In Sweden some years ago, researchers discovered that women as young as eighteen who worked on computer assembly were developing arthritis in their shoulders from maintaining the same position for eight hours a day. So they instituted a system in which a bell would ring at frequent intervals, at which time all the women would move their shoulders in a series of exercises for a brief spell. Not only did the arthritic problems diminish substantially, the incidence of industrial accidents dropped 75 percent within a year.

Everyone has a normal range of motion. It diminishes as a consequence of inactivity. Activity restores it. Joints maintain their nutrition and their youth essentially by virtue of movement. Diminished movement ages the body prematurely.

Anyone who sits in essentially the same posture throughout the day would do well to emulate those Swedish women. Anyone past thirty-five should emulate them as well, whether he or she remains in a fixed position or not. By that age, postural problems will have caused changes in the body that ought to be corrected.

If you've been in a postural slump for any length of time, all the tissues on your front chest wall have shortened. When you want to take a deep breath, you can't because the tissues have tightened up.

The last five exercises—the One-Minute Break—are designed to correct those problems. Take a minute at the end of every hour to do them. They will stretch those shortened muscles. In a relatively brief time, you'll be able to breathe more deeply and stand in a more youthful posture.

All the exercises in this chapter will limber up your body. Like the exercises in the preceding chapter, they should be done every day. Compared to the small investment of time, the payoff is tremendous. That feeling of stiffness will leave your body. Aches and pains will disappear. You'll move once again with an ease that you thought had disappeared from your life forever.

Remember: Slow and gentle movements. Stretch only so far and so long as it's comfortable. The moment a movement becomes uncomfortable, ease off.

SHOULDER STRETCH

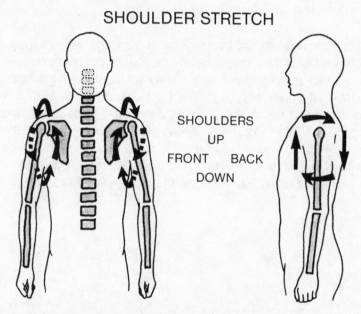

SHOULDERS
UP
FRONT   BACK
DOWN

WITH OR WITHOUT WEIGHTS IN HANDS

This shoulder exercise will improve range of motion as well as posture. Rotate the shoulders in four smooth and continuous movements—first up, then back, then down, then forward. Throughout the movement, hold the head high, chin in. Do five repetitions.

This exercise stretches the muscles of the spine, which benefits both your back and your abdomen. **1.** Raise your right arm over your head, and cross your left arm over your abdomen. **2.** Stretch to the left as far as you can without discomfort. **3.** Hold this position for a count of five. Don't bounce. **4.** Repeat. **5.** Then stretch the other side. Keep knees slightly bent to protect the back. As in all stretching exercises, move slowly as far as you can without discomfort, then hold the position for a slow count of five. Don't bounce. Repeat once, then work the other side.

SIDE BENDING 1

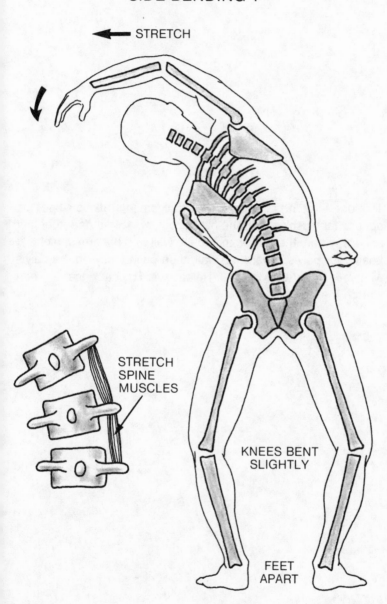

STRETCH

STRETCH
SPINE
MUSCLES

KNEES BENT
SLIGHTLY

FEET
APART

This one stretches the muscles and ligaments of the spine, the abdominal muscles, and the hip abductors. **1.** With feet together and away from the wall, lean into the wall with the arm straight. **2.** Lean your pelvis toward the wall, then push firmly on the pelvis with your other arm. Hold. **3.** Release. **4.** Repeat once. **5.** Then stretch the other side.

SIDE BENDING 2

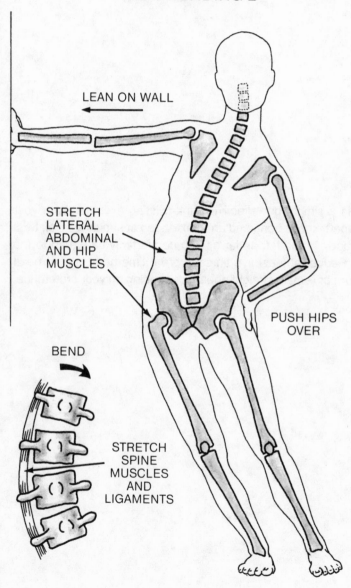

LEAN ON WALL

STRETCH
LATERAL
ABDOMINAL
AND HIP
MUSCLES

PUSH HIPS
OVER

BEND

STRETCH
SPINE
MUSCLES
AND
LIGAMENTS

This is a simple but effective trunk-twisting exercise. With your feet apart, knees bent, and arms extended at shoulder level, twist your body to the left as far as you comfortably can, then to the right. Repeat at least five times, more if time permits. The head can turn or remain straight ahead, depending on your preference.

TRUNK TWIST

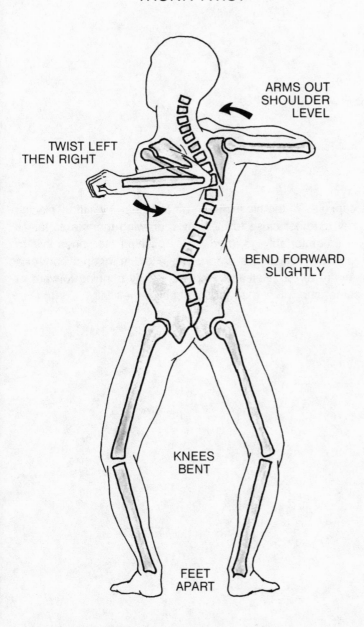

ARMS OUT
SHOULDER
LEVEL

TWIST LEFT
THEN RIGHT

BEND FORWARD
SLIGHTLY

KNEES
BENT

FEET
APART

The capsules of the hip joint can be stretched by sitting, placing the feet together close to the pelvis, drawing them in as far as they will comfortably go, then slowly pushing the knees toward the floor with your hands or forearms. Hold in that position for a slow count of ten. Release. Repeat. Gently bending forward at the same time will stretch the low back beneficially.

HIP STRETCH 1

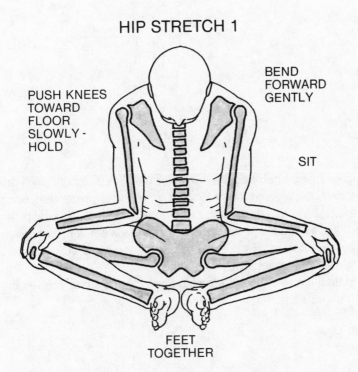

BEND FORWARD GENTLY

PUSH KNEES TOWARD FLOOR SLOWLY - HOLD

SIT

FEET TOGETHER

This exercise stretches the hip flexor muscles. It's done with the low back flat against the ground. **1.** With one leg extended, bring the other leg to your chest, bending at the knee. **2.** Grasp the bent leg as shown, above the knee at the lower thigh, to prevent excessive flexion of the knee. **3.** Hold for a slow count of five. Release. **4.** Repeat. **5.** Change legs.

In addition to stretching the hip flexor, the exercise rotates the pelvis and flattens the low back.

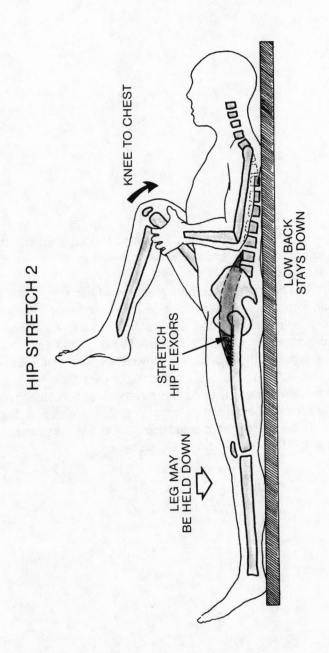

HIP STRETCH 2

KNEE TO CHEST

STRETCH
HIP FLEXORS

LOW BACK
STAYS DOWN

LEG MAY
BE HELD DOWN

This exercise will stretch a much neglected piece of anatomy, the heel cord or "Achilles tendon," while at the same time stretching the calf muscle.

FIRST MOVEMENT: **1.** Place both feet several feet from the wall. **2.** Lean into the wall, supporting yourself with your hands at shoulder level. **3.** Bring one leg forward, bending the knee. **4.** With the other leg straight and the foot flat on the floor, lean forward, pressing the forward knee toward the wall, until you feel a good stretch in the calf. **5.** Hold for fifteen seconds.

SECOND MOVEMENT: **1.** Bring the forward foot back alongside the rear foot and hold it just off the ground. **2.** Move up and down slowly on the ball of the planted foot. **3.** Do five repetitions. **4.** Reverse the feet and repeat the exercise.

HEEL CORD STRETCH

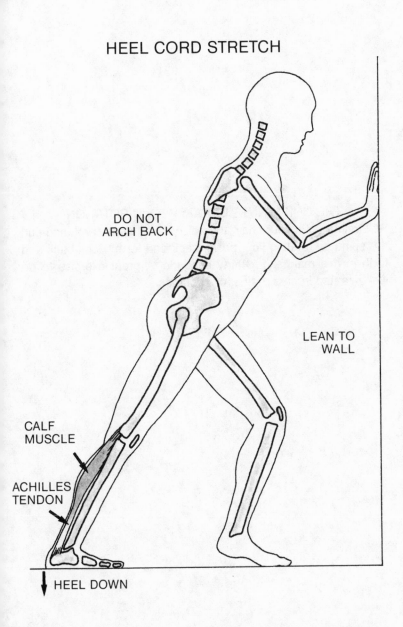

THE ONE-MINUTE BREAK: PELVIC ROTATION

Sit straight up in your chair, then slowly and gently arch and curl the spine by rotating your pelvis back and forth. Rock back and forth in this manner for thirty seconds. A great exercise to do while seated in cars, trains, or airplanes.

THE ONE-MINUTE BREAK:
PELVIC ROTATION

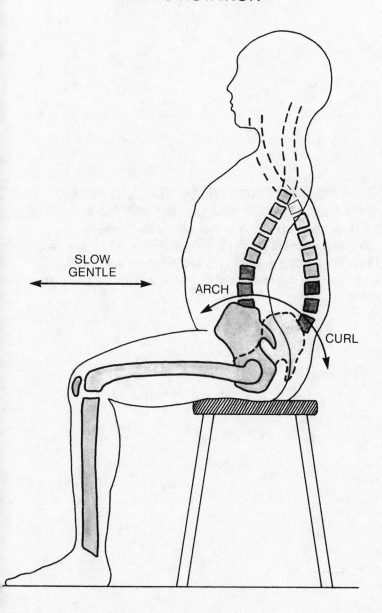

SLOW GENTLE

ARCH

CURL

THE ONE-MINUTE BREAK: STANDING PUSH-UP

Stand at arm's length from an open doorway. With your hands on the door frame at shoulder level, slowly lean forward, chin in, until you feel your chest getting a good stretch. Hold for five seconds. Return to starting position. Do two repetitions.

Repeat the exercise raising and lowering the arms as indicated.

THE ONE-MINUTE BREAK: STANDING PUSH-UP

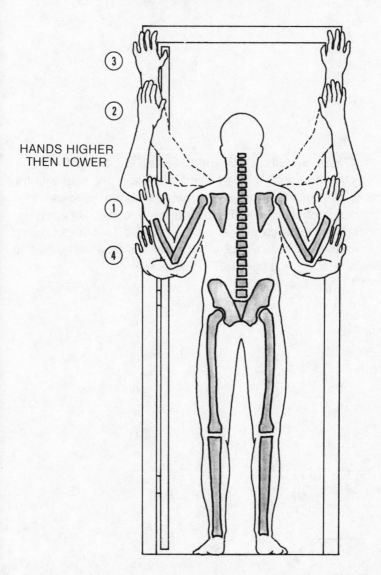

HANDS HIGHER
THEN LOWER

THE ONE-MINUTE BREAK: SHOULDER STRETCH 1
With the arms straight and behind you, grasp one wrist with the other hand and pull both arms slowly back from the spine as far as you comfortably can. Hold for a few seconds. Release. Repeat. Reverse hands and repeat the exercise. Like the preceding exercise, this one stretches all shoulder and chest muscles, and helps flexibility and posture. Do not arch the neck.

THE ONE-MINUTE BREAK:
SHOULDER STRETCH 1

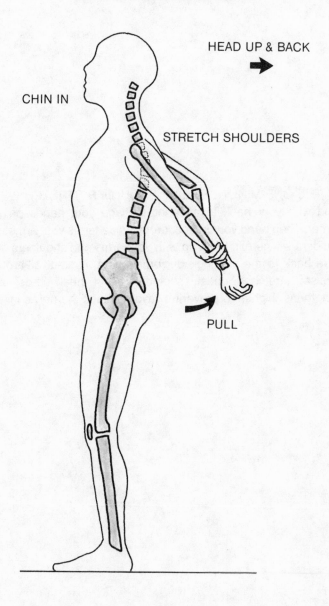

HEAD UP & BACK

CHIN IN

STRETCH SHOULDERS

PULL

THE ONE-MINUTE BREAK: SHOULDER STRETCH 2

Stand with your back to a counter. Place your hands on the counter. Then bend your knees, dropping as far as your arms and shoulders will permit: Push up with your arms and shoulders until you're back to the starting position. Repeat. A great all-around exercise; stretches chest, shoulders, and heel cords, and strengthens thighs. To prevent swayback, tuck the pelvis in.

THE ONE-MINUTE BREAK:
SHOULDER STRETCH 2

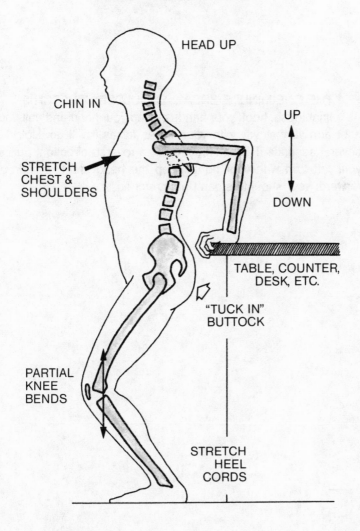

THE ONE-MINUTE BREAK: SHOULDER STRETCH 3

As a final touch, hook your hands behind your head and pull your right arm very slowly with your left as far as it will go. Hold for several seconds. Relax. Repeat. Then reverse direction, pulling your left arm with your right. Keep the head erect. If it drops forward, your shoulders can't be stretched.

THE ONE-MINUTE BREAK: SHOULDER STRETCH 3

HOOK HANDS BEHIND HEAD

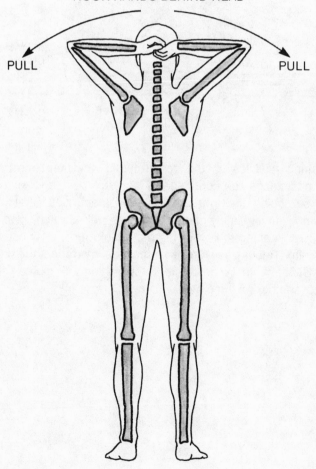

PULL PULL

"PROTECTIVE" HAMSTRING STRETCH

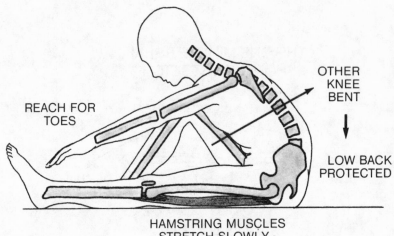

REACH FOR
TOES

OTHER
KNEE
BENT

LOW BACK
PROTECTED

HAMSTRING MUSCLES
STRETCH SLOWLY -
HOLD

Hamstring muscles should be stretched, and kept stretched. Tight hamstrings can contribute to low back pain, and will often pull if stretching does not precede athletic activities. Stretch the hamstrings immediately after athletics as well. Stretch them one at a time, keeping the other leg bent. Hold for a slow count of five. Relax. Repeat. Then reverse the legs and repeat the procedure. Stiffening the knee of the extended leg will enable you to stretch another few degrees.

8. STEP THREE: DEFENDING YOUR BACK

Nothing puts us out of action more effectively than a backache. We can be in fantastic shape in every other respect, but if we develop a backache, it becomes difficult to walk and running is out of the question. All we really want to do is lie down. The sad truth is that most of us at some point will develop a debilitating backache—particularly after the age of thirty-five. It behooves us, therefore, to diminish the likelihood to a minimum, and to have ourselves in such good condition that the damage, if it occurs, will be minimal.

There are three components to the defense of the back:

• The first is to align it properly.
• The second is to make it stronger and more flexible in order to maintain that alignment.
• The third is to maintain that alignment at all times, whether we are standing, sitting, resting, working, playing, or exercising.

All three of these components are equal in importance. If any of them is not present, problems result.

• A person with excellent alignment and good strength and flexibility can injure the back by not using it properly.
• A person with excellent alignment and proper function can injure the back if it isn't sufficiently strong and flexible.
• A person with good strength and flexibility and proper function can injure the back if it's not in proper alignment.

In Chapter 4, we learned how poor posture can produce a low backache, overstretching muscles and tissues, narrowing the distance between the vertebrae on the inside of the spinal curve until they press unduly on the disks and pinch the nerves that pass through the windows of the spine. In Chapter 6, we learned a number of exercises designed to make us "stand tall," thereby decreasing the curves in the spine. So in theory, at least, we now have the motivation to improve our posture and an understanding of the mechanics by which such improvement is accomplished. Now let's add the finishing touches by learning, first, how to make the back stronger and more flexible, and then how to maintain good alignment in everything we do.

Strengthening the Back: The "Air Bag" Theory

We begin with what, to the layperson, may seem like a paradox: The low back is strengthened, essentially, by strengthening the muscles of the abdomen.

I can't think of anyone in the field of physical medicine who would deny that the secret of a strong back is a strong abdomen. But while there is agreement on this point, no one really knows for certain why strong abdominal muscles play such a role, why the right "front" makes the best "back."

There *is* a theory, however. While it hasn't been chiseled in granite, it seems to make sense not only to me but to many of my colleagues. The theory is that the abdominal wall forms one side of an "air bag" within the abdominal cavity, the other three sides of which are the pelvis, the diaphragm, and the spine. The more taut the abdominal muscles, the greater the push against the contents of the abdominal cavity—the intestines, fluid, and air. The greater the push, the more pressure on the curve of the spinal column. Thus the pressure of the abdominal muscles eventually translates into a straighter spine.

THE "AIR BAG" THEORY

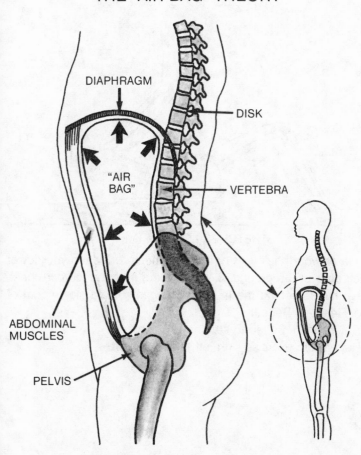

We're fairly certain that the low back is as strong as the abdominal muscles. We're not altogether sure why. Here's one possibility—that the abdominal muscles form one wall of an air bag inside the abdominal cavity, the other walls of which are formed by the diaphragm, the pelvis, and the spine and its muscles. Strong abdominal muscles keep the air bag from sagging. Thus reinforced, the air bag supports the spine.

KNEES TO CHEST 1

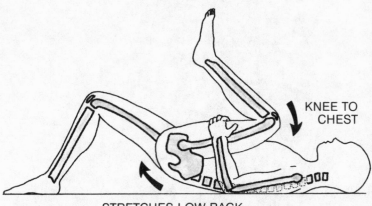

KNEE TO CHEST

STRETCHES LOW BACK

1. Lie on your back with both knees bent. **2.** Flatten your lower back against the ground. **3.** Raise the right knee to your chest, clasp hands behind the leg and pull gently for a slow count of five. Relax. **4.** Repeat.

Return the right leg to starting position.

Repeat the exercise with left knee to chest.

Think of a balloon held between your hands. Press on the balloon with your left hand and you will feel an increase in pressure in your right hand. That, in effect, is what happens when you firm up your abdominal muscles.

The muscles of the stomach assist the back in yet another way. There are two pairs of oblique muscles—so-called because they go off at an angle—that run from around the front of the belly to the spine, where they attach to other muscles. Exercises that

KNEES TO CHEST 2

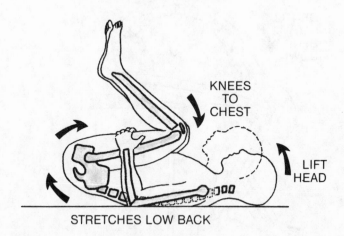

KNEES
TO
CHEST

LIFT
HEAD

STRETCHES LOW BACK

1. Bring both knees to chest, clasping hands behind the legs. **2.** Pull gently and try to lift head between knees. **3.** Hold five seconds and return to the starting position. **4.** Do five repetitions.

stretch the skin of these oblique muscles make them stronger, which further strengthens the back.

When you exercise the low back, it's vitally important that you not overdo it. If you're exercising properly, you'll feel an increasing sense of fatigue, but no pain. The moment you feel discomfort, which is the beginning of pain, you should stop.

You're perfectly capable of distinguishing between an exercise that's helping you and one that's doing you harm. It doesn't take a medical degree to evaluate what you're feeling.

Now to the exercises. First, we'll work on flexibility. Then we'll work on strength.

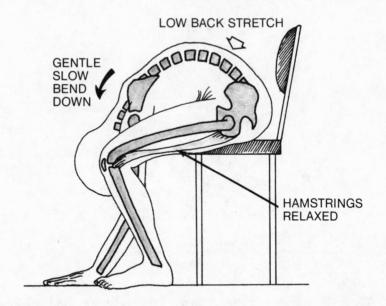

LOW BACK STRETCH

GENTLE
SLOW
BEND
DOWN

HAMSTRINGS
RELAXED

Here's that safe stretching exercise for the low back we talked about earlier. **1.** From a seated position in a chair and with feet and knees apart, bend toward the floor as far as you comfortably can. **2.** Stretch slowly—don't bounce. **3.** Hold for twenty seconds.

The Pelvic Tilt decreases swayback, stretches the tissues of the back beneficially, strengthens the abdominal muscles, and improves posture while instilling a subconscious concept of good posture.

PHASE ONE: Lie on your back, with your knees bent, and press your low back against the floor.

PHASE TWO: Slowly raise the pelvis one or two inches from the floor, keeping the back on the floor, hold for a slow count of five, then return to the floor. Repeat second phase five times.

"PELVIC TILT"

FIRST PHASE

② KNEES BENT   ① LIE ON BACK

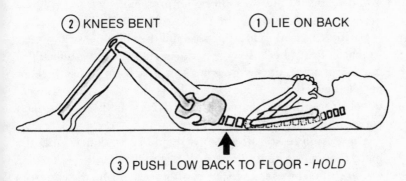

③ PUSH LOW BACK TO FLOOR - *HOLD*

SECOND PHASE

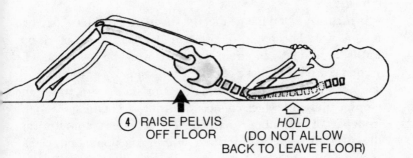

④ RAISE PELVIS
   OFF FLOOR
                      HOLD
               (DO NOT ALLOW
          BACK TO LEAVE FLOOR)

Taking the Sting Out of Sit-ups

Many people gag involuntarily when a doctor puts a tongue depressor in their mouth to look down their throat. When that happens, I fault the doctor, not the patient. If he'd just tell his patient to sing a note and hold it, the muscles of the tongue would relax and there would be no problem.

We have something of the same problem with sit-ups.

Mention a sit-up to most people and they become sick to their stomach. That's because conventional sit-ups can be difficult, if not impossible, for anyone who's not used to doing them or hasn't done them in years. And almost invariably, it's conventional sit-ups they're taught. If any of this sounds familiar, fault your gym teacher, not yourself.

There is no reason why sit-ups should be so difficult that the mere thought of doing them makes you ill.

Our sit-up comes in five stages, progressing from the easiest to the hardest stage. The first stage is so simple that any healthy person can do it, no matter how out of shape he or she is. The fifth stage is a pretty fair test of fitness.

If you're completely out of shape, start with Stage One, and move to each successive stage when the previous one becomes too easy.

In each stage, you'll note that the knees are bent. There are two reasons why. The first is to protect your back; attempting sit-ups with straight legs can strain the muscles of the low back. The second reason is to make certain it's the muscles of the stomach and not the hips that are getting the workout. In any sit-up, the iliopsoas muscles, which connect the front part of the spine to the front part of the hipbone, participate to an extent. But by raising the knees, their role in lifting and lowering the upper body can be considerably reduced.

Remember, once again, that the benefit you receive from an exercise is relative to the condition you're in when you begin. If

SIT-UP: STAGE 1

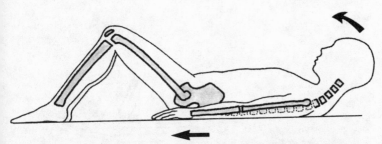

Sit-ups strengthen the abdominal muscles and the low back. There are five stages, each progressively more difficult. Perform at whatever level is comfortable for you, advancing to the next stage when you can.

STAGE ONE: 1. Begin the exercise lying on the floor, with your arms at your sides and your knees bent. **2.** Lift your head from the floor as far as you comfortably can. At the same time, slide your hands toward your feet. **3.** Hold for a slow count of five. **4.** Return to the starting position. Relax. **5.** Do as many repetitions as you can until mildly fatigued.

SIT-UP: STAGE 2

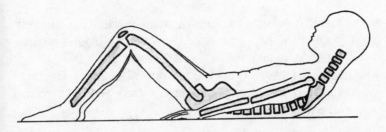

STAGE TWO: 1. Assume the same starting position as in Stage One. **2.** This time, slowly lift your head and your shoulders as high as you comfortably can. At the same time slide your hands along the floor toward your feet. **3.** Hold for a slow count of five. **4.** Return to the starting position. Relax. **5.** Do as many repetitions as you can until mildly fatigued.

SIT-UPS: STAGES 3, 4 & 5

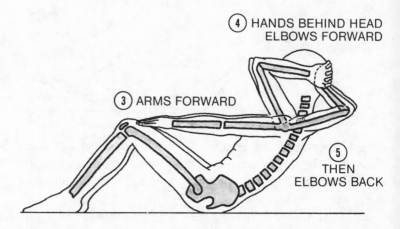

④ HANDS BEHIND HEAD
ELBOWS FORWARD

③ ARMS FORWARD

⑤
THEN
ELBOWS BACK

STAGE THREE: 1. Assume the same starting position as before. **2.** This time, "peel" your back off the floor by raising the vertebrae in stages, to approximately forty-five degrees. As you do, keep the arms forward and parallel to the ground. **3.** Hold for a count of five. **4.** Return to the starting position. Relax. **5.** Do as many repetitions as you can until mildly fatigued.

STAGE FOUR: 1. Assume the same starting position, but lace your hands together behind your head. **2.** With your elbows pointing forward, rise to an angle of forty-five degrees, again by "peeling" your back from the floor. **3.** Hold for a count of five. **4.** Return to the starting position. Relax. **5.** Do as many repetitions as you can until mildly fatigued.

STAGE FIVE: 1. Assume the same starting position as before, but hold your elbows back as far as they will go. **2.** Rise to an angle of forty-five degrees, again by "peeling" your back from the floor. **3.** Hold for a count of five. **4.** Return to the starting position. Relax. **5.** Do as many repetitions as you can until mildly fatigued.

you're in your fifties, sixties, seventies, or eighties and haven't done a sit-up in years, you'll probably gain a larger percentage of fitness from doing Stage One sit-ups than a well-conditioned person will gain from working out at Stage Five.

The Last Ingredient: Function

You've learned to "stand tall." You know how to strengthen your back and maintain its flexibility. Now for the third, and final, ingredient in the defense of the back against injury: proper function.

We've said that proper alignment, strength and flexibility, and proper function are all vital components of a sound defense. The truth is that if you did nothing but maintain proper function you'd be way ahead of the game. All the exercise in the world, together with exquisite alignment, are of no value if you don't sit, stand, lie, or lift in a safe and sound manner.

Ninety percent of the human race who are disabled can blame it on low back pain. Eighty percent of disability claims are based on low back problems, according to insurance statistics. Billions of dollars are spent to treat low back injuries; pennies are spent on the prevention of such injuries.

The two main culprits are overuse and misuse. Either will injure ligaments, muscles joints, and the disks of the spine, resulting in pain and functional impairment. It's all so unnecessary. All that's needed to prevent a majority of low back problems is a little knowledge and a little thought. Once you know what to do, you have to think about what you're doing.

Sitting. Considering the amount of practice we get, you'd think that we'd develop into proficient sitters. The fact is that most of us don't sit well at all. The fault isn't entirely ours. Chairs of the same type are all built to approximately the same height, even though the heights of humans vary. Ideal sitting means that the

ISOMETRIC SIT-BACK
STAGE 1

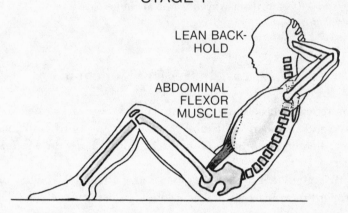

LEAN BACK-
HOLD

ABDOMINAL
FLEXOR
MUSCLE

ISOMETRIC SIT-BACK
STAGE 2

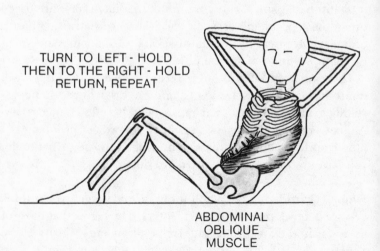

TURN TO LEFT - HOLD
THEN TO THE RIGHT - HOLD
RETURN, REPEAT

ABDOMINAL
OBLIQUE
MUSCLE

thighs should be slightly elevated—tough to do if you're less than average height. One remedy is a stool or hassock for the feet. Another remedy, if your chair is adjustable, is to lower the height —which will not only keep your knees higher than your hips but also cause you to sit up straighter.

In the ideal sitting position, you're sitting on your pelvis, balanced on the two bony prominences called *ischia*. If your weight is ahead of the ischia, it arches the low back—no good. If your weight is well behind the ischia, you're slumping—also no good. The proper position is with the weight slightly behind the ischia.

This exercise strengthens the oblique abdominal muscles, which begin at the front of the body and move obliquely around the trunk, attaching to the spinal erector muscles of the back. Recent research has established that these are the muscles that give the most support to the lower back. Every time you exercise these muscles, you make the skin of the muscle tougher.

To do the exercise: **1.** Wrap your feet around a sturdy post, or hook them under a chair or bed. **2.** With your knees well bent and your hands laced behind your head, elbows out, curl back until you feel your abdomen tighten, and hold the position for five seconds. **3.** Turn your upper body to the right as far as you can and hold five seconds. **4.** Turn to the left as far as you can and hold five seconds.

Do as many repetitions as you can until mildly fatigued. If the exercise is too difficult, lean forward; as the exercise becomes easier, lean back. Pointing the elbows forward will also diminish the stress.

Isometric sit-backs produce low back pain in some people usually because they lean straight back instead of curling back. If such pain persists, eliminate this exercise and do graduated sit-ups instead.

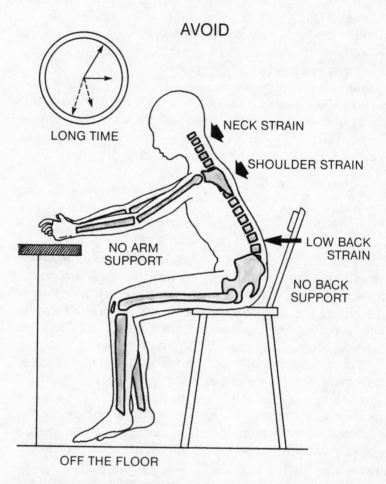

AVOID

LONG TIME

NECK STRAIN

SHOULDER STRAIN

NO ARM
SUPPORT

LOW BACK
STRAIN

NO BACK
SUPPORT

OFF THE FLOOR

Prolonged sitting in a bent forward posture places strain on the neck, low back, and shoulders, particularly if the arms aren't supported and there is no back support. Feet off the ground add to the strain.

IDEAL SITTING

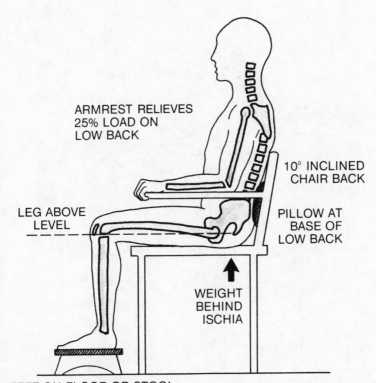

ARMREST RELIEVES
25% LOAD ON
LOW BACK

10° INCLINED
CHAIR BACK

LEG ABOVE
LEVEL

PILLOW AT
BASE OF
LOW BACK

WEIGHT
BEHIND
ISCHIA

FEET ON FLOOR OR STOOL

To sit properly, keep your weight slightly behind the *ischia,* the bones of the pelvis you can feel when you sit. If the weight is too far forward, your back is arched; if too far back, you're slumped. A *slight* slump, supported by a thin pillow at the very base of the low back, is ideal. A ten-degree incline in the chair back provides ideal support; so do armrests, which decrease weight on spine by 25 percent. Use a stool or hassock under your feet; it will elevate the thighs.

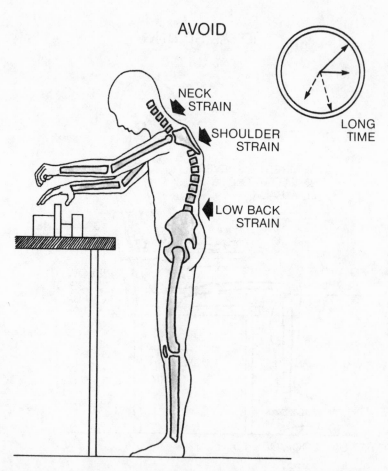

AVOID

NECK STRAIN

SHOULDER STRAIN

LOW BACK STRAIN

LONG TIME

Bending over while standing for a prolonged period at the stove, sink, or drawing board strains the ligaments of the neck and low back and fatigues the muscles of the neck, shoulders, and low back. Ultimately, the muscles give up; overstretching results.

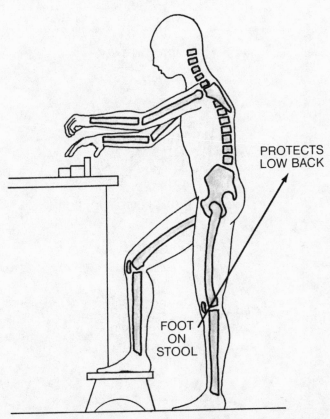

PROTECTS
LOW BACK

FOOT
ON
STOOL

Whenever you're working at a sink or counter for protracted periods, you can take a great deal of strain off your low back simply by placing one foot on a stool or box.

LIFT PROPERLY

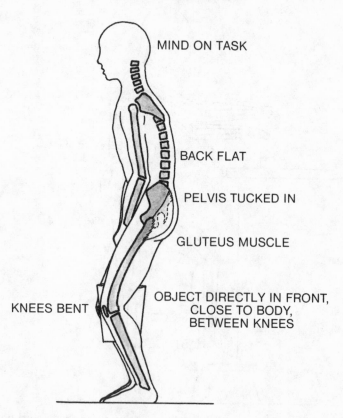

MIND ON TASK

BACK FLAT

PELVIS TUCKED IN

GLUTEUS MUSCLE

KNEES BENT

OBJECT DIRECTLY IN FRONT,
CLOSE TO BODY,
BETWEEN KNEES

Rules for lifting: (1) mind on the task, (2) lift slowly, (3) object
directly in front of you, (4) object close to body, preferably between knees, (5) knees bent, (6) pelvis tucked in. Practice frequently until proper movement is second nature.

PROPER WAY TO LIFT WHEN OBJECT TO ONE SIDE

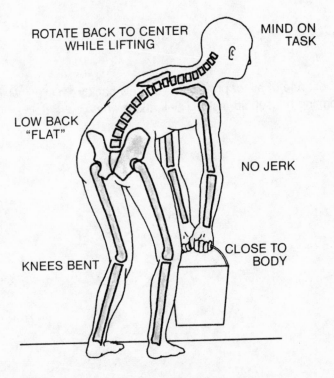

ROTATE BACK TO CENTER WHILE LIFTING

MIND ON TASK

LOW BACK "FLAT"

NO JERK

KNEES BENT

CLOSE TO BODY

To lift an object that's to one side of you:
1. Bend forward. 2. Turn to the side. 3. Grasp the object. 4. Turn back to the front. 5. Straighten. Never attempt to lift while the trunk is rotated.

The best rule of all for protecting your low back from injury while performing household tasks: Think about what you're doing.

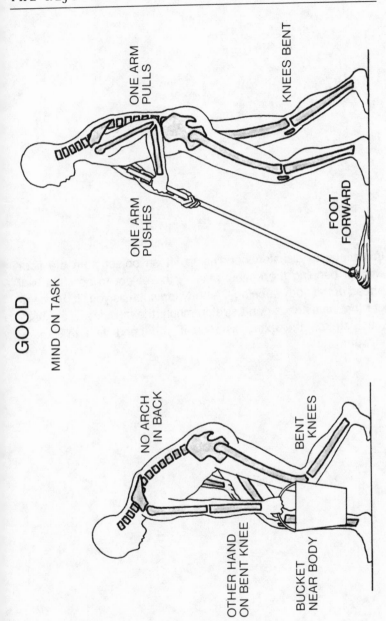

GOOD

MIND ON TASK

ONE ARM PULLS

ONE ARM PUSHES

KNEES BENT

FOOT FORWARD

NO ARCH IN BACK

BENT KNEES

OTHER HAND ON BENT KNEE

BUCKET NEAR BODY

Invitations to disaster: bending to lift an object from the floor without bending the knees; placing the object to be lifted well ahead of the body; arching the body too soon as you lift. Remember that hamstrings don't stretch much; the muscles of the back must stretch the extra distance if you bend with the knees straight.

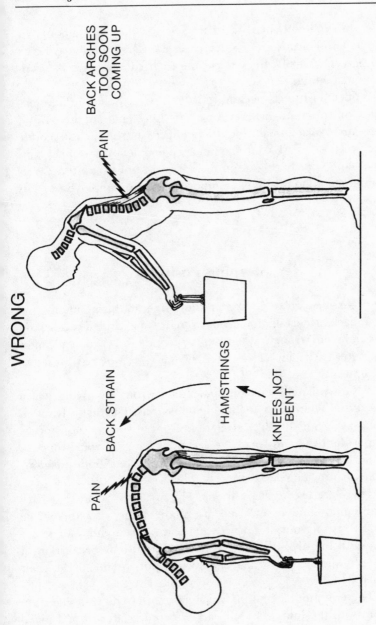

WRONG

A thin pillow behind the back ensures the right amount of curve. Using arm supports decreases the weight on the spine by 25 percent. Finally, the back of the chair should slope back approximately ten degrees.

Proper posture is needed in the office, at home, in automobiles, on airplanes—wherever we sit for any length of time. Don't hesitate to take a small stool to the office, so that you can elevate your feet, or to ask your maintenance people for a proper chair. You—and your back—are in that chair for hours at a time; your continued good health is as important to your employers as it is to you.

Sleeping Positions

Let's assume you've done everything right to this point: aligned your back, stood tall, done your exercises, and drilled yourself on the right and wrong ways to stand, sit, and lift. Do you still suffer from low back pain? If so, the chances are that you're sleeping in an unhealthy position.

Nature will tell you you're sleeping wrong by giving you a backache. There are two "wrong" positions. The first is lying on your back with your legs straight in front of you and no support under the head and legs. The second is lying on your stomach, either with your legs straight or one leg flexed. Both positions accentuate your swayback.

There are two right positions. The first is lying on your back with a pillow under your head and another under your knees. The second is on your side with your body curled and your knees bent. Of the two, the latter is preferable, if only because most people who sleep on their backs won't put a pillow under their knees.

There is another reason, which has more to do with digestion than with the low back. Millions of people suffer from a hiatal hernia, which prevents a tight seal from forming between the esophagus and stomach and thus permits gases to move back up through the esophagus. Enough gas can cause serious inflammation of the tissue, which in turn can produce an esophageal obstruction that can impede the passage of food. Any action that will help evacuate the stomach of food most rapidly will minimize the formation of gas as well as its movement back into the esophagus. By sleeping on your right side you're employing gravity in the best possible manner. Gravity helps move the food from the stomach to the duodenum.

If you're one of those people fortunate enough not to have a hiatal hernia, you can sleep on either side without a problem—although your digestion will still be assisted by sleeping on your right side.

In the morning, get out of bed in stages. If you're not already on your side, roll over. Then draw your knees up and gradually come up sideways, pushing yourself to a sitting position as your legs swing to the floor. To stand, bend forward at the waist until your shoulders are directly above your knees, then slowly straighten. If you don't move the torso forward first, you can't avoid arching the back when you stand—something you don't want to do.

Turn a Good Lesson into a Good *Habit*

A story in the Los Angeles *Times* in the late summer of 1984 had a beautiful lesson buried in its body type. The story was about a man who coached older amateur athletes to become better at their sports. The coach talked about the application of Zen Buddhism to improvement, particularly to the manner in which it helps his performers focus on their task. "Zen," he said, "is the art of doing what you're doing."

I have never heard it put better. I can't think of an aspect of life to which it doesn't apply, from the most philosophical notion of learning to fully experience each moment of life to the most practical application of thinking about each task.

Learning a lesson won't do you a bit of good if you don't consciously attempt to work it into your life. Sitting, standing, lying, and lifting are such simple tasks, done so often every day that we must force ourselves to think about them if we want to replace bad habits with good ones.

To paraphrase that coach: "Do what you're doing."

9. STEP FOUR: GETTING STRONG

We lose strength as we age. The loss is inevitable, because we lose muscle fibers as well as their chemical components. At sixty years of age, we won't have the strength we had at forty-five even if we could do all the things we were doing at forty-five to maintain our strength, the reason being that we'll have fewer muscle fibers to work with. As we noted earlier, of the billion or more fibers with which we began life, we'll have lost millions. *But* we'll still have millions to work with—which will more than answer our needs provided we work them in a constructive manner. What's more, exercise decreases the natural evolutionary loss of muscle fibers. The final point to remember is that if you have come to exercise late in life following an essentially sedentary existence—and if you are doing more at sixty to build your strength than you were doing at forty-five—you *can* be stronger at sixty than you were at forty-five.

The primary importance of strength may well be psychological. More than bulk and even endurance, it gives us confidence in ourselves. But strength is also an important functional component of everything we do. Without it, many simple tasks become impossible, among them standing, sitting, even sleeping. (Without strength we couldn't turn in bed.) Strength is what keeps our body parts in place.

Weak or tired muscles will produce undesirable changes in the body's lever system, which usually leads, in turn, to injuries, particularly to the knees, hips, and hamstrings. If three quarters of all recreational runners will eventually be sidelined by injuries, one major cause is the lack of sufficient and balanced strength.

To gain strength, you will want to employ the principle of *overload:* The load or force you move, the number of repetitions, or the speed of your effort must be greater than the previous effort if you're to gain a fitness benefit. That's not as grim a prospect as it seems; as your physical condition improves, you're able to overload with no more effort than you expended at the start of the program.

There are two major ideas here; it's important that you have a clear understanding of both. The first is that you must constantly increase the challenge. The second is that the increased challenge will always be surmounted with no more effort than easier tests were accomplished at the outset.

Suppose that after years of doing nothing, you were asked to carry two pails filled with water a distance of a hundred yards. Your first effort would exhaust you. You might have to stop several times. The next morning your body would ache. But after one week of exactly the same exercise, you would accomplish it with relative ease, and probably without setting the pails down once. Nor would your muscles ache the morning after.

The example offers several lessons: First, it demonstrates how quickly the body adapts to a challenge. People who are unfit to begin with show the most dramatic gains of anyone at the outset of a training program. A 50 percent gain in fitness in a matter of six to eight weeks can easily be achieved. Second, the example offers proof of the importance of adding to the task in order to gain a fitness benefit. If you keep doing the same thing in the same way, it soon becomes so easy that the body isn't stimulated to a beneficial degree. To add to your fitness level—to gain strength—you would have to add extra water to each pail, or carry the pails a greater distance, or cover the same distance in a shorter period.

Warming Up and Warming Down

In Chapter 5, we talked about the need to warm up before we stretch, to get the blood flowing into the muscles. In Chapters 6 through 8, we learned a number of stretching exercises designed to rejuvenate tissue, particularly in those areas of the body that are especially vulnerable to aging. Taken together, these exercises are an excellent warming up routine to be used both before and after physical activities, be they sports or conditioning.

Because it's so important, let's restate the case for warming up before an activity. Inactivity causes the crisscrossing fibers in tissue to adhere to one another at the junction points. In this condition, any abrupt or vigorous movement could cause the tissue to tear. What frees the fibers up is body heat—warm blood surging through the body's vessels and into the extremities. The best way to get the blood moving is to move all the body parts in a slow, steady and gentle manner for ten to fifteen minutes. That— as we'll see in Chapter 11 when we put all the exercise routines together into a comprehensive program—is about how much time it takes to complete the stretching routine.

Most people readily accept the logic of warm-ups, and are reasonably faithful about doing them, or at least making a pass at doing them. But almost no one except dedicated professional and amateur athletes bothers with "warm-downs," as postexercise stretching exercises are known. Yet warm-downs are every bit as important as warm-ups.

Exercise irritates muscles. All sorts of waste products, such as lactic acid, substance P, and prostaglandins accumulate in fatigued muscles, irritating the nerve endings. This irritation causes the muscles to contract reflexively. Only by stretching an exercised muscle immediately after exercise can this neurological reflex action be intercepted and stopped. Only then can the muscle relax.

Push-ups strengthen the shoulders, chest muscles, arms, and back. They can be made easy or difficult, depending on your condition. **1.** Start, if necessary, by pushing away from a wall. **2.** With your feet a yard from the wall, extend your arms and let yourself fall forward until your hands touch the wall. **3.** Bend at the elbows until your head almost touches the wall. **4.** Return to the starting position. **5.** Repeat until moderately fatigued. To increase the difficulty, move to a table counter, then a chair, preferably one with armrests, which will permit you to lower the body farther, thereby increasing shoulder flexibility. When this push-up becomes too easy, move to the floor, extending the body but bending the knees so they touch the ground. When you have sufficient strength, you can do the push-ups with your legs straight, and when you're really strong, you can elevate your feet so they are higher than your head. In all positions, be sure to keep your buttocks slightly elevated to prevent arching of the back.

PUSHUPS

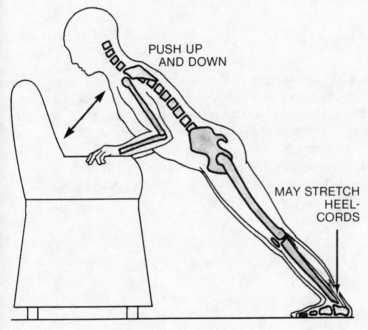

PUSH UP
AND DOWN

MAY STRETCH
HEEL-
CORDS

Dips strengthen and stretch the muscles of the upper back, arms, and shoulders. **1.** With your feet on the floor, place your hands, palms down, on the armrests or seat of a chair. **2.** Stretch your legs in front of you. **3.** Lower your body as far as you can while bending the arms. **4.** Return to the starting position. **5.** Repeat as many times as you comfortably can. To increase difficulty later, put your feet on a second chair or a coffee table.

DIPS

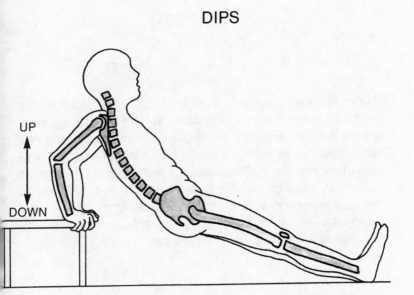

This exercise will strengthen the quadriceps, the muscles in your thighs. It's also marvelous for posture. **1.** Put your back against a smooth door, a refrigerator, or a secure wall mirror. **2.** Place your feet a few inches from the surface. **3.** Flatten your low back against the surface. **4.** Slide down the surface until your legs are bent at an angle of forty-five degrees—no farther. **5.** Return to the starting position. **6.** Repeat until moderately fatigued. Another excellent exercise, especially for skiers, is to maintain the forty-five-degree angle for as long as you can.

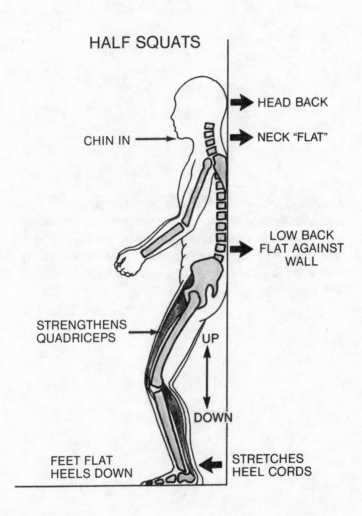

HALF SQUATS

HEAD BACK

NECK "FLAT"

CHIN IN

LOW BACK
FLAT AGAINST
WALL

STRENGTHENS
QUADRICEPS

UP

DOWN

FEET FLAT
HEELS DOWN

STRETCHES
HEEL CORDS

Another good quadriceps exercise, particularly for those with knee problems. If you don't have weights, you can drape a purse over your ankle, or wear a ski boot or other heavy shoe. Keep the raised leg straight, the other bent at the knee and hip, which keeps the low back from arching. Build up to twenty repetitions with each leg.

QUADRICEPS EXERCISE

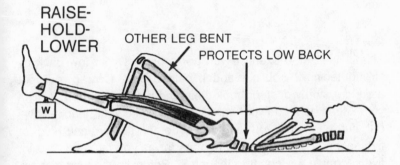

RAISE-
HOLD-
LOWER

OTHER LEG BENT

PROTECTS LOW BACK

W

This is the same exercise you do to protect your low back by strengthening the oblique abdominal muscles. **1.** Wrap your feet around a sturdy post, or hook them under a chair or bed. **2.** With your knees bent and your hands laced behind your head, elbows out, curl back until you feel your abdomen tighten, and hold for five seconds. **3.** Turn to the right as far as you can and hold for five seconds. **4.** Repeat to the left. **5.** Return to the starting position. Work up to five repetitions of the exercise. To increase difficulty, lean back; to decrease, lean forward.

ISOMETRIC SIT-BACK
STAGE 1

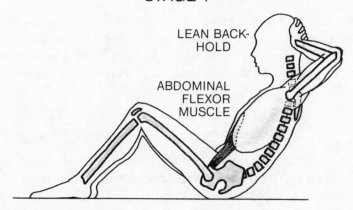

LEAN BACK-
HOLD

ABDOMINAL
FLEXOR
MUSCLE

ISOMETRIC SIT-BACK
STAGE 2

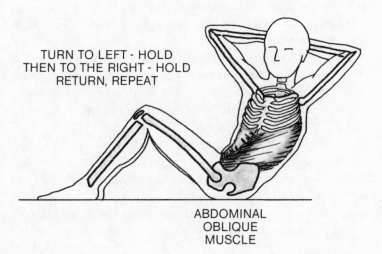

TURN TO LEFT - HOLD
THEN TO THE RIGHT - HOLD
RETURN, REPEAT

ABDOMINAL
OBLIQUE
MUSCLE

We're all familiar with the tightness and stiffness that follows a bout of heavy physical activity. If you engage in slow sustained stretching after such activity, you can avoid most or all such problems. The basic rule is to concentrate on stretching those parts you're already "feeling" as a consequence of your activity. But it's a good idea to stretch the other muscles, as well.

The routine will be presented in Chapter 11. For now, it's enough to remember that warm-ups and warm-downs should bracket physical activity—including the following strength exercises:

Strength vs. Power:
Some Thoughts for Recreational Athletes

Now let's suppose you've gotten yourself into shape. What's next? If you're anything like the rest of us, you'd probably like to translate that enhanced physical condition into improved performance on the tennis court, the golf course, the ski slopes, or wherever your passion leads you. How important is strength at this point, and how much time should you devote to increasing it? The answer may surprise you: Strength is of only secondary importance in most sports.

Strength is nothing more than the ability to do work. Expressed as a formula, Strength equals Force times Distance. There's no time factor involved. You can be very strong—and very slow. All the strength in the world won't help you where a need for quickness is involved.

And where isn't quickness involved? It's a factor in almost every recreational sport: tennis, racquetball, basketball, volleyball, baseball, even cycling, running, and swimming. In fact, the only sport in which quickness isn't a significant factor is weight lifting—the very activity that most efficiently builds up strength.

Does this mean that you shouldn't continue to build up your

strength? Not at all. What it means is that strength ought to be placed in perspective. It's a component of another capacity that, once you're reasonably fit, might be much more pertinent to your needs. That capacity is *power*.

Power is the ability to apply strength very quickly. Expressed as an equation, Power equals Strength divided by Time. It's power you need to move between two points—for example, to get from where you are to where your opponent has hit the ball. Carl Lewis, America's premier track and field Olympian, is a sublime exponent of power. When he takes off from the long jump board, it's with a single burst of explosive power. One of these days, Lewis will probably move farther from that board to a point in the long jump pit than any human has before. He'll need strength to do it, but without the addition of power, he might not make it into the pit.

It's not the lack of strength but the lack of power that keeps otherwise talented collegiate players from making it in the National Football League. A lack of power, not a lack of strength, could also be detracting from your prowess as a recreational athlete.

How, then, do you develop power?

The body recruits muscle fibers for each event. It takes neurological training to accustom the muscle fibers to the demands that will be made on them. The professionals call such training *specificity*. What it means is that you train in the mode, with the specific motions, and *at the speed* characteristic of your event.

Suppose you're a tennis player. If you move slowly during practice sessions, your muscle fibers won't be trained to respond efficiently when you summon them to carry you at greater speeds during your match. When you want to sprint for a ball on a crucial point, unless you've trained for it by sprinting in practice, 60 percent of your muscle fibers will have no idea what's going on.

Performance power is improved only when you train your muscles at a speed equal to or greater than that of the event. If you're spending six hours a week lifting weights in a gym to increase your strength on the assumption that it will help you in your event, you had better ask yourself whether your time could be put to better use.

Strength is a vital but limited component of athletic performance. If you want to enhance that performance, you have to make time for power training.

The Power Workout

Transforming a strength workout to a power workout is simplicity itself. Just work faster—attempting to do many more repetitions of each exercise in a given amount of time. If you were doing all the foregoing exercises for thirty seconds each—an excellent interval, incidentally—the more repetitions you did during each thirty-second interval, the more you would transform the circuit (all the exercises) into a power workout.

Normally, you would want to rest for one minute between each exercise. But if power's what you want, gradually cut the rest interval until you're working out *and* resting for thirty-second periods.

Finally, remember to stretch before and after each strength or power workout.

10. STEP FIVE:
WALK, DON'T RUN, TO FITNESS

We arrive now at what, both literally and figuratively, has become the heart of all fitness programs: the conditioning of our cardiovascular system.

A strong heart *ought* to be the heart of a fitness program. Without it, everything else is irrelevant.

What is a strong heart? It's one that beats as infrequently as possible and with the greatest force each time. Each powerful contraction pushes the blood out of the heart and into the bloodstream.

There is absolutely no doubt that exercise is extremely important in the development of a strong heart muscle. Like any other muscle, the heart must be used to be stimulated. If it isn't stressed beyond its normal resting rate, it will react as any muscle does and weaken from disuse.

When you exercise, your heart beats faster. This stress not only gives the heart a beneficial workout but pumps blood through the blood vessels at a rate that tones them up and carries off impurities as well. The effect is something like that of running water at high speed through clogged and rusted pipe. To a certain extent the pressure will help free the passages.

But the most important factor is what's called "stroke volume," the amount of blood displaced by each contraction of the heart. The more blood displaced by each stroke, the more efficient the heart.

Now, how do you achieve a strong heart? What form does the

exercise take, and how should it be monitored? How do you know when you've exercised the heart sufficiently? Without trying to unnecessarily dramatize the matter, I would have to say that these are life-and-death questions. You owe it to yourself to consider the answers carefully, without simply accepting the conventional wisdom on faith.

Heart-Rated Exercise: How Valid?

Over the last decade, we have seen a great increase in the popularity of what has come to be called "heart-rated" exercise. Through a series of simple calculations, each person can figure out a "target heart rate," the number of beats per minute to which he or she tries to elevate the heart rate. While there are several formulas, generally speaking the figure is reached by subtracting one's age from 220 (the theoretical outer limit of heartbeats per minute) and then multiplying that figure by 60 percent if one is unfit, 70 percent if moderately fit, and 80 percent if very fit.

Examples:

An unfit person of thirty-five would exercise at a target heart rate of 111 beats per minute ($220 - 35 = 185 \times .60 = 111$).

A moderately fit person of forty would exercise at a target heart rate of 126 beats per minute ($220 - 40 = 180 \times .70 = 126$).

A very fit person of fifty would exercise at a rate of 136 beats per minute ($220 - 50 = 170 \times .80 = 136$).

The beats are monitored by taking one's pulse for six seconds and then adding a zero. Thirteen beats in six seconds would translate to 130 beats a minute, fourteen beats to 140 beats a minute, and so forth. The matchup of formula to practice need not be exact; if your formula result is 126, you can safely exercise in the range of 120–130 beats a minute.

The thesis underlying heart-rated exercise is a good one: It's the only way you can know, scientifically, exactly what kind of stimulus your body is receiving from your exertions. As exercise becomes progressively easier, you could perform the same routine without giving yourself an adequate workout. Each time you exercised, your heart would receive less of a challenge than the previous time and soon lose condition. Using a target heart rate, on the other hand, would require you to work harder as your condition improved in order to increase your heartbeat.

There are a number of reasons, however, why I am not enamored of heart-rated exercise, particularly for older people.

In the first place, there is no completely accepted body of scientific evidence indicating that the formula used to calculate heart rates is the right one to maintain maximum cardiovascular condition. I am reminded of the standards used for years to determine ideal weight. These standards were arbitrarily set up by the insurance companies, based on longevity data they had acquired over the years indicating that thin people lived longer than fat people. Today, the tables have been revised to the extent that it's now "okay" to weigh ten to fifteen pounds more than previously thought advisable.

I have read all the literature and discussed the matter with my cardiologist colleagues and I am simply not persuaded that they have made a compelling enough case to warrant setting this method up above all others.

One of the problems with heart-rated exercise is that, as simple as it is, it is sometimes misunderstood by those who administer it. A friend of mine who is familiar with the concepts told me the following horror story. He had gone to an aerobics class one day at a popular health club. The class was led by a superbly conditioned young woman not more than twenty. In the class were several men in their forties, and two men in their fifties, all of them at least twenty pounds overweight. After a prolonged bout of intense exercise, the young woman stopped, directed the attention of her class to a wall clock and shouted, "Count your pulse . . . now." Six seconds later she shouted, "Stop! Okay, any eighteens?" Two of the portly men raised their hands. "Good!" she cried. "Any seventeens?" Two others raised their hands. "Good!" she cried again. "Sixteens?" And so on. When she finished her inventory, she said, "Okay, you twelves and thirteens, keep working and you'll get your count up there."

After the class, my friend quietly sought out the manager and suggested that he educate his aerobics instructor or face the likelihood that someone in her class would expire on the spot.

What had the young woman done wrong? In the first place, it is extremely dangerous to completely stop one's motion immediately after an arduous bout of exercise. When you do that, the blood pools up in the lower extremities, and chemicals build up in the blood that momentarily raise blood pressure, producing an incredible strain on the heart. But much more worrisome is the total misunderstanding of heart-rated exercise exhibited by the young woman. The objective is *not* to raise your pulse rate as high as you can. It is to raise it to a level appropriate for your age and condition. The men in their fifties had elevated their heart rates forty to fifty beats a minute higher than they should have been. The men in their forties were at least thirty beats above a safe level for them.

I have no quarrel with anyone who makes intelligent use of a pulse-rated exercise program. To the contrary, the idea of monitoring one's own bodily response to exercise can serve as an inducement, an elementary and easily performed biofeedback exercise. My concern is that monitoring the pulse will be perceived as a requirement by many persons who aren't interested in doing so and will be used in turn as an excuse to avoid cardiovascular exercise altogether.

For the dedicated and disciplined person, there is no problem. For others, pulse-rated exercise could add yet another obstacle to participation—too technical, too time-consuming, too boring. Actually, it is none of these, but to those looking for an excuse, it could easily be: one more standard to achieve, one added possibility of failure.

There is also something off-putting in the idea that you benefit from exercise only if you raise your heart rate to a level calculated by a precise formula. I, for one, don't happen to believe that.

I have never checked my pulse during a lifetime of exercise. I don't need a pulse check to tell me whether I'm having a vigorous workout. I can tell, and not just because I'm a doctor. The indications are evident to anyone.

- Your heart beats faster; you can feel it.
- Your breathing is quicker; you can hear it.
- You heat up; your skin becomes moist.
- After a while, you begin to feel exhilarated.

When you stop, you feel an afterglow, a sense of well-being, that lasts for several hours.

My point isn't that heart-rated exercise doesn't work. It does work. My point is that it's not really necessary if you don't want to bother. You have the sensibility to determine whether you're getting a benefit out of your workout without taking your pulse. For those concerned, dedicated, scientifically astute people who want to be precise about their response to exertion, fine, let them equate their fitness to a numerical coefficient. But I don't think you have to equate fitness with numerical value—the single exception being if you have some form of cardiovascular disease and must be careful not to stimulate your heart beyond a certain level. Suppose you never measured your pulse but were able to do everything that you wanted to in life with ease and comfort, without stress or fatigue. You would consider yourself perfectly fit without ever knowing what your pulse rate was when you exerted yourself.

Make no mistake: *You must exert yourself.* You must feel and hear and see the signs of exertion, and maintain your effort until you're pleasantly fatigued. But in my opinion, you don't have to elevate your heart rate so precisely—or experience the physiological destruction to the rest of your body that jogging, the most popular form of heart-rated exercise, so often produces.

The High Cost of Jogging

Some years ago, a researcher in orthopedics did a study with rabbits that was painful to read about but of great significance to humans. His first step was to surgically damage the cartilage in the hip joints of a number of rabbits—the identical injury in all cases. Then he divided the rabbits into three groups. The first group of rabbits was allowed to run freely on the damaged joints. The damaged joints of the second group were placed in casts so that the joints could not be moved. The rest of the rabbits were suspended in hammocks with their legs dangling, with a mechanical device attached to the limbs of the damaged joints in such a manner that the limbs were continuously moved. At no time, however, did the joints bear weight.

A few months later the researcher sacrificed the animals and studied their hip joints. Those whose hips had been put in a cast showed no cartilage regeneration at all, and were going through all the ravages of arthritis. The rabbits that had been permitted to run free had begun to regenerate cartilage, although very, very little. The third group of rabbits, those that had been suspended from hammocks but had their joints moved, had made a remarkable recovery. Their cartilage had regenerated beautifully.

The lessons learned from rabbits are readily applicable to humans: Movement is essential to maintain the health of joints; weight bearing is detrimental beyond a certain point.

The ideal exercise, therefore, would be one that embodied a great deal of movement with a minimum of weight bearing. That would be rapid walking or bicycling or swimming or even cross-country skiing. It would most definitely not be jogging.

There's no doubt whatever that jogging benefits the cardiovascular system. But this benefit has to be weighed against the profound muscular and skeletal deterioration that may result, particularly after thirty-five.

You can get away with jogging when you're younger because young tendons and ligaments are far more resilient than they will be after thirty-five. Young people, furthermore, tend not to be as heavy as older people, which means less weight bearing down on their cartilage. And young people tend to move faster than older people, with a longer stride, the body leaning forward and the weight borne on the balls of the feet and cushioned by the calf muscles. Jogging, by comparison, is done in a much more upright position than running, with the body more over the feet, the back more arched, and more weight bearing directly down on the feet, knees, and hips. Running presents no problem for young people; it would prevent far less of a problem than jogging for older people, provided they could manage it. Far better to run in short bursts, with periods of walking in between, than to jog methodically and uninterruptedly for the same period of time or distance.

Let's look at the damage that jogging can produce:

The foot. It hits the ground nine hundred times per mile with two to five times the body weight. Thus, a hundred-pound woman could be putting as much as five hundred pounds of weight on her foot with each forward stride. The bones of the foot are like a complex jigsaw puzzle of tiny pieces; they just can't take such punishment. To complicate matters, as we age, our feet tend to pronate, or point out, which makes them much more vulnerable to stress. They become floppier, less flexible, and flatter. Such tendencies are of little consequence when we stand or walk, but once we begin to jog, these defects are magnified. The arch flattens further; the impact on the heel is sizably greater, just as it is on the ball of the foot. Where there was once a cushiony flesh pad to absorb the shock, both the heel and the ball of the foot have flattened out over time from all the wear and tear, and both spots become inviting targets for injury. Worse yet, the impact separates those tiny bones.

Another not uncommon problem is the "heel spur." To understand how it develops, think of the foot as a bow and the tissue on the sole of the foot as the string of the bow. As the foot flattens,

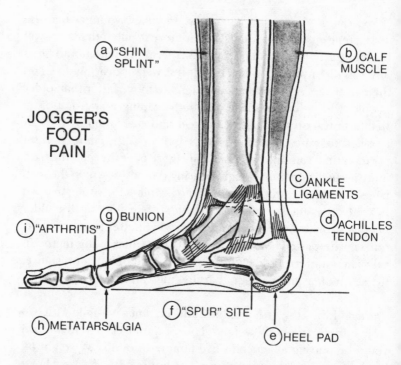

JOGGER'S FOOT PAIN

(a) "SHIN SPLINT"
(b) CALF MUSCLE
(c) ANKLE LIGAMENTS
(d) ACHILLES TENDON
(g) BUNION
(i) "ARTHRITIS"
(h) METATARSALGIA
(f) "SPUR" SITE
(e) HEEL PAD

The possibilities of damage to the foot and lower leg from jogging are legion: (a) shin splints, pain in the front of the lower leg caused by strain, (b) pain in the calf from overuse or overstretching, (c) pain in the ankle ligaments of unbalanced feet, (d) an inflamed or torn Achilles tendon, (e) a heel pad worn from too much pounding, (f) a spur, especially in flat feet, (g) bunions, usually from poorly fitted shoes, (h) pain in the balls of the toes, especially in flat or pronated feet, and (i) arthritis in the toe joints, especially when the toes are not perfectly aligned.

that string gets stretched. Normal stretching is good for it; undue stretching, such as that experienced hundreds of times while jogging, can cause it to begin to pull away from the heel bone, where it's attached at one end. As the tendon pulls the bone skin away, nature fills that void, first with scar tissue, eventually with bone. That bone is the heel spur. When you step on it, it feels as if a nail has been driven into your foot.

For any or all of the above reasons, problems can develop. It hurts to walk, or even to wear shoes; nerve pains shoot into the legs.

One frequently hears the advice that if you get a special pair of shoes, or use arch supports, or lose weight, or run a little faster, you can diminish the effects of the impact. All such advice has a measure of truth to it, but none of these measures can by themselves ensure you against injury. Very rarely are they successful.

The knee. As we jog, the kneecap rides up and down nine hundred times a mile, absorbing a force five to *nine* times the body weight at each stride. Under such duress, the ligaments and cartilage in the knee become strained, damaged, and torn. Swelling, tenderness, and arthritic changes can result. It becomes difficult to get out of a chair, go up and down stairs, or even walk.

Jogging isn't bad for every knee. If you're fortunate enough to be one of those persons with absolutely straight legs, you can probably jog without ill effect providing you don't overdo it. But if your legs have a minor discrepancy from the norm, jogging will magnify the difference until it becomes a problem. An outright malalignment or a defect will compound the problem greatly.

Suppose you're knock-kneed. It's a common enough characteristic, and not in the least unsightly. Yet a knock-knee throws the entire mechanism of the leg out of alignment. Ideally, when the foot strikes the ground the knee is directly above it. When you're knock-kneed, the foot is outside the knee. As you jog, the force propels the kneecap out of its normal socket each time the knee bends and straightens. The action can produce degenerative changes in the kneecap and knee joint. Eventually the kneecap can wear out.

The hip joint. The leg fits into the hip like a ball into a socket. Jogging can so damage that fitting that arthritis of the hip results.

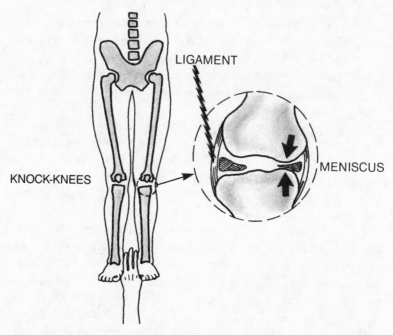

If you're a knock-kneed jogger, you're straining the inner ligaments of your knees, crushing the outer meniscus (a cartilage within the joint) of each knee, and slipping—and possibly dislocating—the kneecap, or patella. If three fingers can be slipped between your ankles while your knees are touching, you're knock-kneed.

Then it's painful to stand, let alone walk. (See illustration, page 21.)

The low back. As we've seen, it's built like a compression system, cushioned by sponges called disks. When we jog, we not only unduly squeeze the disks, but also arch the back, which puts stress on the facet joints at the back of the spine. Enough squeez-

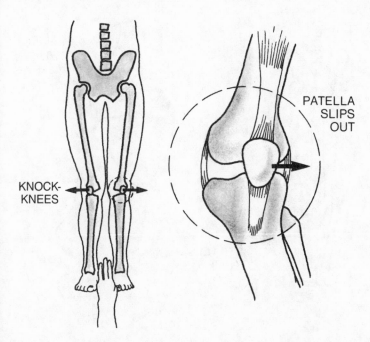

KNOCK-
KNEES

PATELLA
SLIPS
OUT

Repeated bending can dislocate the patella of the knock-kneed
jogger.

ing of disks and rubbing of cartilage on cartilage and both disks
and joints wear out. Result: great pain, and loss of function.

If You Insist on Jogging . . .

I can guarantee you, sight unseen, that you would be far better off
to engage in almost any activity other than jogging to stimulate
your heart. Bicycling, swimming, strenuous walking are all better
for the body than that constant pounding. At the same time, I
know what a joy jogging can be and how important it becomes to

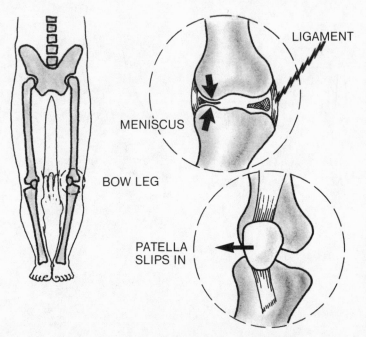

For the bowlegged jogger, the hazards are the mirror image of those for the knock-kneed jogger: a strain on the outer ligaments of the knee, excessive pressure on the inner portion of the knee joint and the inner (medial) meniscus, and the possibility that the kneecap, or patella, will slip to the inside and dislocate. A three-finger space between the knees with the ankles together indicates bowlegs.

its adherents. So if you are one of them, and you don't want to stop, let's at least equip you with the information you need to be certain you're not producing the kind of bodily changes that could sideline you altogether from jogging or any other sport. Bear in mind that one person in two has some minor abnormality in structure that can be greatly magnified by jogging.

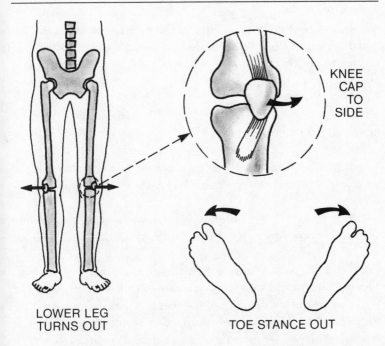

LOWER LEG
TURNS OUT

KNEE
CAP
TO
SIDE

TOE STANCE OUT

Joggers who run with their toes out force their lower legs to twist out, causing knee joint and kneecap pain, and forcing the kneecap to the outside.

First test: the hips. Make certain that your hips are perfectly competent to take the strain of weight bearing. You can determine this far better than any doctor, simply by observing your performance.

• Both hips should be free of pain when you stand.
• You should be able to walk at a reasonably good clip without a limp.
• You should be sufficiently flexible in the hip joints. To determine if you are, sit on the floor and draw the legs toward you

with the soles of the feet together. Push down on your knees with equal pressure. Both legs should go down an equal distance. If one leg will not go down as far as the other, it's an indication of an abnormality in that hip.

Next test: the legs. The object is to determine whether you're knock-kneed or bowlegged.

- If you can place three fingers between your ankles while your knees are touching, you're knock-kneed. (See pages 164–65.)
- If you can place three fingers between your knees while your ankles are touching, you're bowlegged. (See page 166.)

Final test: the feet. Standing normally, look down at your feet. Ideally, they would be almost parallel to one another, with the toes turned out six degrees. If the feet are slightly supinated, or turned in, you don't have much to worry about. If, however, the feet are pronated, or turned out, more than six degrees, you're in a weak position. You can get away with it while walking, but jogging causes the pronated foot to roll to the inside, thereby magnifying the stress. The pronated foot makes the arch flatten down even more than normally when you jog, and puts added stress on the knee.

If you're not certain whether your feet are pronated, wet them and walk on concrete. The pattern will be unmistakable.

If you're pronated and you still want to jog, by all means use molded orthotic supports in your shoes. Better yet, try the exercise of my choice, the simplest, best exercise there is.

Walking: Safe, Simple, and—Done Right— More than Enough for the Job

Bicycling is great exercise. So is cross-country skiing. So is swimming. In none of these activities is there the kind of weight-bearing shock produced when you jog. But bicycling requires equipment and safe streets or paths; cross-country skiing requires equipment, snow, and travel, and swimming requires a pool—formidable obstacles to all but the dedicated or lucky or rich. Walking presents no such obstacles.

The overwhelming majority of people will benefit greatly from the added stress placed on their hearts by vigorous walking. As a measure of insurance, however, I strongly recommend a stress test, administered by a cardiologist, to anyone embarking on any exercise program, particularly if the activity will be in marked contrast to a sedentary past. Even those athletes and exercisers who consider themselves to be in excellent physical condition would do well to take periodic stress tests at intervals recommended by their physicians. Jim Fixx, the author-runner, died while jogging in 1984; had he taken a stress test, as he'd been advised to because of the history of heart disease in his family, he might be alive today.

Stress tests are simple, safe, and painless. You move on a treadmill at an accelerating rate for up to fifteen minutes, while electrodes pasted on your body broadcast the body's response.

Please don't read anything more than a physician's prudence into my recommendation in behalf of stress tests. Walking—even accelerated walking—is the safest exercise I know.

I walk for an hour almost every morning in a manner that exercises not only my heart but my entire body. When for some reason I can't walk for several days, I feel sluggish. My weight, normally no problem for me, begins to increase. And my disposition deteriorates. More about these conditions in the next few chapters. For now, I want to argue—as vigorously as I can—that walking, *vigorous* walking, is the best possible exercise for anyone past thirty-five. It gives you an excellent cardiovascular workout without punishing your body.

Normal walking won't do the job. You must walk rapidly *and* you must employ your entire body.

One of the problems with jogging, aside from its potential to inflict injury, is that it doesn't utilize the upper body. All the

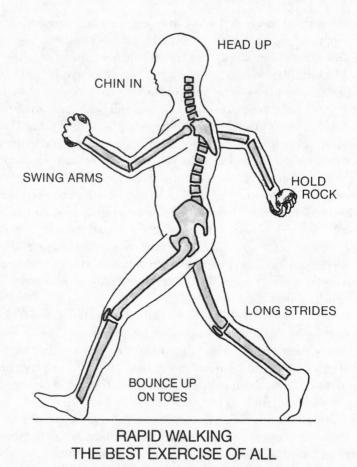

HEAD UP

CHIN IN

SWING ARMS

HOLD ROCK

LONG STRIDES

BOUNCE UP ON TOES

RAPID WALKING
THE BEST EXERCISE OF ALL

Brisk, sustained walking is the best possible all-around exercise for cardiac, pulmonary, and general conditioning without fear of injury. Start by walking at a clip of 3 miles per hour—20 minutes per mile. Gradually increase to 4 miles per hour—15 minutes per mile. If it's not too arduous, increase still further to 5 miles per hour—12 minutes per mile. Try to walk for at least 30 minutes 3 days a week; ideally, you would walk each day for an hour. Rule: It's better to walk a shorter distance at a faster rate than a longer distance at a slower rate.

strain in getting your heart rate up is placed on the muscles of the legs. But upper body muscles, properly engaged, can contribute greatly to your workout. Certain symphony orchestra conductors are a fine example of this. They live a tension-filled life, yet many of them live a very long time. Toscanini was ninety when he died. Stokowski signed a new, eight-year employment contract at the age of ninety-five, and fulfilled half of it. Neither man ever exercised formally, to my knowledge. They didn't have to. They got all the exercise they needed simply by moving their upper bodies each day. No doubt their sense of fulfillment contributed to their longevity. Heredity may have been a factor, too. But a good measure of credit has to be given to the auxiliary support they developed for their heart muscles by all that waving of the arms.

Every muscle in the body is something of an auxiliary heart. Each pumps blood in the process of contracting. The upper body has major muscle groups in the shoulders, arms, and back. Using these muscles will get your heart rate up without hurting your joints. In the process you'll give yourself an excellent flexibility workout.

When you walk, you should twist your torso from side to side, and swing your arms. If that effort isn't enough to make you exert yourself, try holding a rock in each hand. The younger you are, the more vigorously you're going to have to move in order to exercise your heart adequately. Relative to your age, however, the perceived effort will seem the same. At forty-five you won't have to walk or move your arms as vigorously as you did at thirty-five in order to receive an exercise benefit. At fifty-five you'll move more slowly still. But in all cases, the benefit relative to your age and condition will be the same.

Practice Good Walking Habits

At every age, you should walk with rapid strides—rapid relative to your normal walking gait—and you should walk with a little bounce so that you strengthen the muscles of your calves and feet.

Walk with posture in mind—body erect, head up. Walk "tall." Use this period to train yourself to walk more efficiently. As we

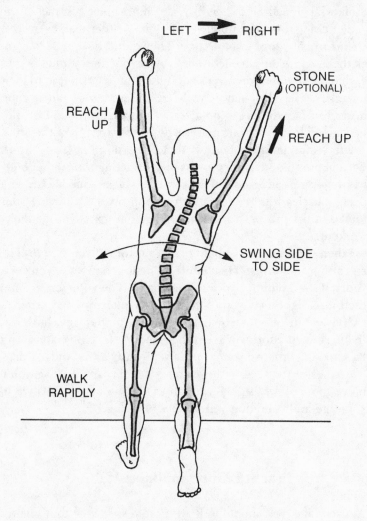

LEFT   RIGHT

REACH UP

STONE
(OPTIONAL)

REACH UP

SWING SIDE
TO SIDE

WALK
RAPIDLY

WALKING-PLUS

age, we tend to turn our toes out, seeking better balance. The more this tendency develops, the more inefficient we become, and the greater the risk that we will loosen the jigsaw-puzzle pieces of the foot. If we pronate at every step, and we take 1,800 to 2,000 walking steps per mile, we'll have that many ligament strains every mile. With that amount of strain, foot fatigue will be the least of our problems.

While stationary feet are ideally placed when pointing out six degrees, once you begin to move the feet are best protected when supinated, with the toes turned slightly in. The faster you walk, the more readily you can do that.

A good walking shoe is mandatory. There are dozens of good brands to choose from. Look for these features: a snug heel, a longitudinal arch on the inner side, good padding under both the heel and the balls (metatarsal heads) of the foot. Molded orthotics, or extra padding, are both good ideas. When you're being fitted, take several minutes to walk around the store at a good clip. You should have the feeling that the shoes are helping your feet to supinate.

If at all possible, walk in areas where automobile traffic is either light or nonexistent. In my travels around the country, I'm always saddened by the sight of runners, joggers, and even walkers taking their workouts along crowded metropolitan arteries—be it

Don't just walk. Walk dynamically, with a rapid gait, a bounce to your step, and total involvement of your torso. Twist and bend your torso; swing, raise, and cross your arms. Do windmills, first backward, then forward. Hold a small stone in each hand to add to the challenge, promote extra cardiac and pulmonary conditioning, and increase flexibility and strength. Walking up inclines further increases conditioning benefits, but should be introduced gradually and only after a vigorous walking program on level ground has sufficiently prepared you for the added exertion.

the FDR Drive in New York, or Lake Shore Drive in Chicago, or Sunset Boulevard in Los Angeles. Whatever aerobic benefits they're obtaining have to be diminished by the deep draughts of carbon monoxide they're taking into their lungs.

The ideal time for your walk would be early in the morning, when carbon monoxide levels are lowest. You'll also benefit from lower temperatures, and avoid dehydration. But don't exercise on an empty stomach; have some juice or fruit first.

Now, what kind of schedule should you maintain? It depends on the benefit you want. The greater the effort, the greater the benefit—so long as the effort is within your ability to tolerate it. It takes longer to get the same aerobic benefit from walking than it does from jogging; the faster you walk, the more you'll diminish that gap. As a rule, walk shorter distances at a faster pace in preference to longer distances at a slower pace.

At a minimum, you would want to walk three times a week for at least thirty minutes each time. But that's truly a minimum. Ideally, walk for an hour each time—rapidly for the first twenty minutes, leisurely for the next twenty minutes, rapidly for the final twenty minutes.

To spur you on your way, keep in mind that rapid walking a specific distance burns more calories than jogging the same distance because you take more steps per minute and thus employ more muscular activity. And because more of the body is involved in rapid walking, particularly when you engage your upper body, it firms the body more than jogging does.

I sometimes hear the complaint that walking is boring. It can be boring only if you're bored with yourself. What better time to sort your thoughts, solve problems, come to decisions? What better time to reflect on life itself, or to meditate, or to simply relax in motion?

11. PUTTING IT ALL TOGETHER: THE REJUVENATION PROGRAM

In the preceding chapters, you've learned the theories behind the process by which body tissue is rejuvenated, and you've become familiar with the physical movements employed to achieve such change. It's time now to put it all together, to lay out the day-by-day program that will help you reverse the aging process.

Along with this program, I am obliged to convey some feelings. I'm not a great believer in the regimented life. I don't like to impose schedules on others, if only because no one, no matter how compulsive, can ever adhere perfectly to a schedule, and lapses, when they inevitably occur, can produce feelings of guilt. The last thing I want is to make you feel guilty as you follow your rejuvenation program. If that were to happen, you might understandably put an end to your feelings by giving the program up.

What a shame that would be—because you really are only weeks away from feeling and looking younger.

The program that follows will help you rejuvenate your body to the extent that you employ it. It has been devised with the objectives of busy men and women in mind. The number of exercises has been reduced to an absolute minimum. So has the number of times you are asked to repeat each exercise. While any effort is better than none at all, your gains will be much more impressive if you follow every procedure without missing a day than they will be if your effort is sporadic. And once you have mastered the program, you'll be that much farther ahead if you increase the number of "sets" of each exercise, and the number of repetitions in each set.

By incorporating portions of the rejuvenation program into your daily life, you will cut down on the amount of time you will need to devote exclusively to it. You *will*, however, need to set aside a short period each day for the program. Once you are familiar with the routines, your workout will become much more efficient, and what might require forty-five to fifty minutes at the outset will be accomplished in thirty or thirty-five.

Remember always that your primary objective is to rejuvenate body tissue, which means that when you are stretching you must at all times move slowly and gently—not only to maximize your benefits but to minimize the possibility of injury.

Remember, too, that the body's temperature is at its lowest point during the waking day on arising, which means that you must take care to heat it up before executing any vigorous movements. I repeat: Morning is not the best time to exercise in terms of the body's preparation for it. But, realistically, it's the best time for most of us because it's the only time we'll do it.

I strongly recommend that you perform your rejuvenation program in a warm-up or sweat suit, rather than in shorts and a T-shirt, so that your warm-up exercises will more efficiently heat your body. If, after the warm-up exercises, you still feel creaky, repeat them a few more times until you loosen up. If you're one of those people who's so stiff in the morning that you can hardly move, take a hot bath or a shower *before* your workout. One way or another, try to raise your body temperature before stretching, and never—repeat, *never*—perform any movement that hurts.

Once your body feels warm, and you can move with ease, you can remove your warm-ups or sweat suit if you become uncomfortably hot. You gain no benefit from undue sweating and, in fact, lose energy.

Those of you who have not been involved in any fitness program or activity prior to this will want to be the most cautious of all, particularly at the outset. As your condition improves, you can graduate your effort.

Once more: Gauge your effort to the response you want, bearing in mind that the choice is yours. In that spirit, here is your seven-days-a-week rejuvenation program:

The Rejuvenation Warm-up Routine—Daily

What you'll accomplish in this routine is to awaken your body as well as your mind, filling it with a good store of oxygen, contracting, then relaxing your muscles in order to generate the flow of blood and restore flexibility, limbering important muscle groups that have grown stiff during the night.

This routine is absolutely essential whether you intend to exercise later or not. It should be performed each morning before you leave your bed.

1. Take three to four deep breaths, breathing from your belly.

2. Lift your head from the pillow.

Hold it briefly.

Lower your head, until it's touching the pillow once again.

Turn your head to the left as far as you can, then to the right.

Return to center.

Repeat five times.

3. Tense all your muscles slowly (Isometric Tension).

Hold for a count of five.

Repeat five to ten times.

4. Bend both your legs to a forty-five-degree angle. Bring one knee to your chest, wrapping your arms under the knee and pulling gently until you sense the low back being stretched.

Repeat with the other knee.

Bring both knees to the chest. Once again, pull gently until you feel a stretch.

Return to the starting position.

Repeat five times.

5. Roll over onto your side, then sit up, placing your feet on the floor.

Bend forward with your arms dangling toward the floor. Feel your back stretching, but don't attempt to stretch beyond what's comfortable.

Hold for a count of ten.

Slowly return to starting position.

Slowly twist your trunk, first to the left, then the right, holding for a count of five at each extreme.

Return to starting position.

6. Move your trunk forward until your shoulders are over your knees.

Stand.

7. Raise up on your toes five times.

The Rejuvenation Warm-downs—Daily

Do these exercises briefly immediately after any strenuous workout or sport.

1. Heel Cord Stretch

Lean against a wall, keeping heels down, and very slowly lean into the wall one leg at a time.

2. Hamstring Stretch

Sit on the floor, with one leg straight and the other bent. Lean forward as far as you comfortably can, touching the toe of the outstretched leg if possible.

Reverse legs and repeat stretch.

3. Hip Stretch

Place soles of feet together, drawing them toward pelvis as far as they'll comfortably go.

Slowly push knees toward floor with hands or forearms.

Hold, gently bending forward.

4. Second Hip Stretch

Lie on back, with the low back flat against the ground.

With one leg extended, bring other leg to chest bending it at the knee and holding it under the knee.

Hold, until you feel a good stretch.

Repeat exercise with legs reversed.

5. Low Back Stretch

Seated in a chair or on the edge of a bed, and with legs and feet separated, drop head and torso between the legs, as far as you can.

Hold, until you feel a good stretch.

6. Forward Bend

From a standing position with legs straight, bend forward, letting your head and arms hang down, until you feel a good stretch. DO NOT TRY TO TOUCH YOUR TOES. Bend your knees before returning to standing position.

7. Shoulder Stretches

Clasp your hands behind your back and pull them away from your back as far as you can.

Repeat several times.

With head erect, clasp hands over your head, and slightly behind it, and pull them from side to side several times.

8. Neck Stretches

With the head erect and facing forward, drop it toward the right shoulder as far as you can, then toward the left shoulder. Repeat several times.

Turn the head from side to side, dropping the chin to the shoulder at the end of each turn.

You're finished—ready to shower, dress, eat a hearty breakfast, and march through the day, standing tall and with a spring to your stride. With good reason: you're already physiologically younger than you were before you began.

That is not hyperbole. It is scientific fact.

The Rejuvenation Stretching Routine—Daily Warming Up

1. ISOMETRIC TENSION

Lying on the floor, tense every muscle in your body as hard as you can. Hold for a count of five. Relax. Repeat five times.

2. BICYCLING

Lift your legs and buttocks into the air, supporting your buttocks with your arms. Pedal slowly to a count of twenty-five, if you can make it; less if you can't. As your stamina increases, pedal to a count of fifty or more. Remember: This is a warm-up exercise. Gentle movements.

BEDROOM BICYCLING

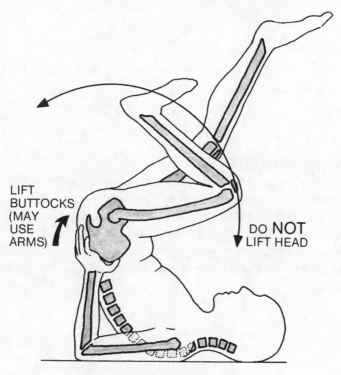

LIFT BUTTOCKS (MAY USE ARMS)

DO **NOT** LIFT HEAD

3. SWINGING WARM-UP

With knees flexed and feet spread, clasp your hands together and slowly swing them over your head and then through your legs, bending at the waist and knees in the process. Repeat fifteen to twenty times without interruption. As your condition improves, you may wish to hold a light weight in your hands and increase the number of repetitions. Remember: Gentle movements.

SWINGING WARMUP

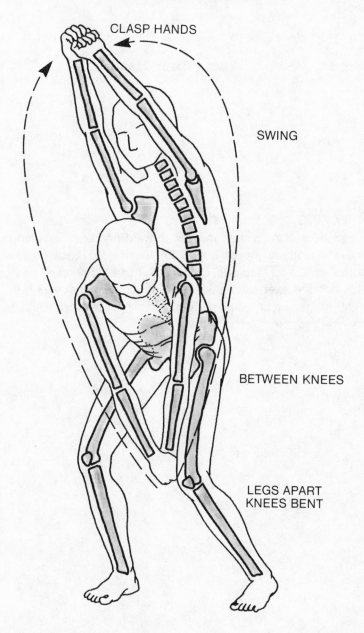

CLASP HANDS

SWING

BETWEEN KNEES

LEGS APART
KNEES BENT

Using Your Head

1. PECKING

Tuck your chin in, then move it forward and back as though sliding it along a greasy board. Emphasize the back position more than the forward one, holding the head momentarily in the back position after each repetition. For variation, turn your head slightly to the left or the right. Do at least five repetitions. (And do this exercise often throughout the day.)

HEAD FORWARD AND BACK-HOLD

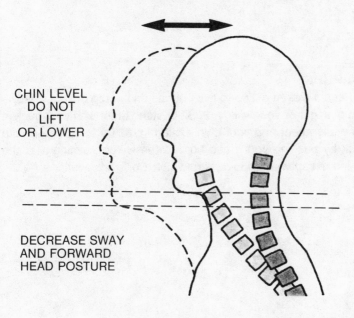

CHIN LEVEL
DO NOT
LIFT
OR LOWER

DECREASE SWAY
AND FORWARD
HEAD POSTURE

2. LIFTING

1. Place a weight of two to five pounds on the top of your head. A bag of sugar or flour will do. **2.** Sit or stand erect with your neck in good alignment and your chin tucked in. **3.** Try to elongate your neck by pushing your head up into the weight, aiming it at the ceiling. Keep your shoulders down. **4.** Do five repetitions.

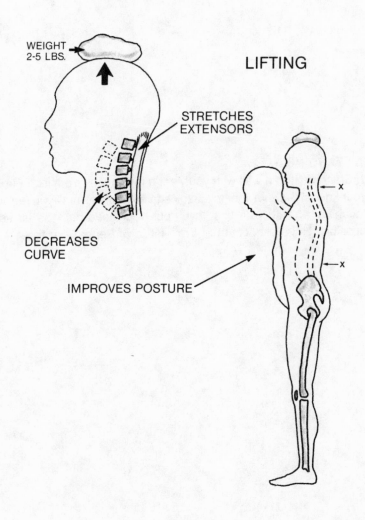

WEIGHT
2-5 LBS.

LIFTING

STRETCHES
EXTENSORS

DECREASES
CURVE

IMPROVES POSTURE

x

x

3. STANDING TALL

1. Stand next to a wall with your feet a few inches from it. **2.** Flex your knees. **3.** Drive your low back against the wall until you feel it touching. **4.** With your chin level, pull your head back as far as possible. Hold for a count of five. Relax. **5.** Repeat five times.

STANDING TALL

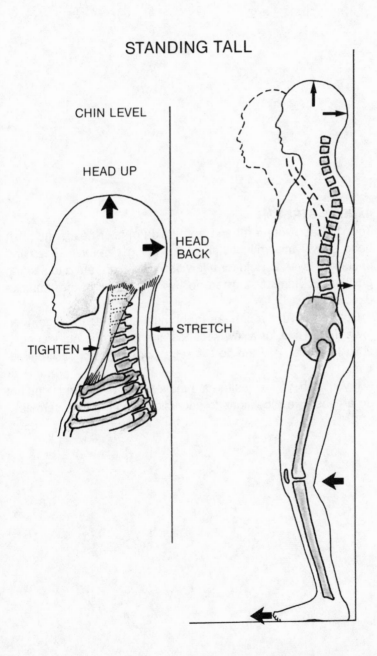

4. NECK STRETCH

Top: **1.** Place your left hand at the side of your head, and push head slowly toward right shoulder, being careful to keep the shoulders level. **2.** Hold for a few seconds, then return to starting position. **3.** Repeat. **4.** Then do two repetitions in the opposite direction.

Bottom: **1.** Turn your head to the right as far as it will go, then lower it. **2.** Hold for a few seconds, then return to starting position. **3.** Repeat. **4.** Then do two repetitions in the opposite direction.

If you wish, you may alternate movements to left and right, but do at least two repetitions to each side—more if time permits.

NECK STRETCH

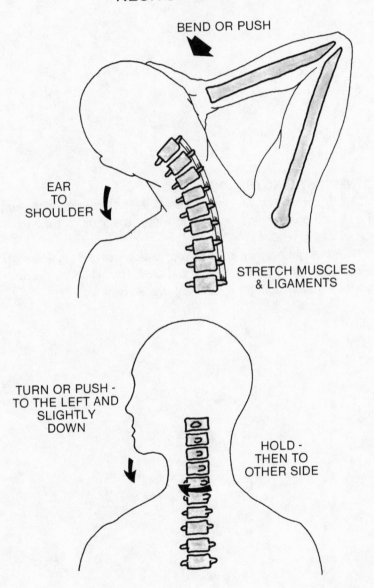

BEND OR PUSH

EAR
TO
SHOULDER

STRETCH MUSCLES
& LIGAMENTS

TURN OR PUSH -
TO THE LEFT AND
SLIGHTLY
DOWN

HOLD -
THEN TO
OTHER SIDE

5. NECK STRENGTHENING 1

1. Place both hands on your forehead. **2.** Push forward with your head, and push against your head with your hands. **3.** Hold for a count of five. Release. **4.** Repeat.

1. Place your hands behind your head, lacing the fingers. **2.** Push backward with your head, and push against your head with your hands. **3.** Hold for a count of five. **4.** Repeat.

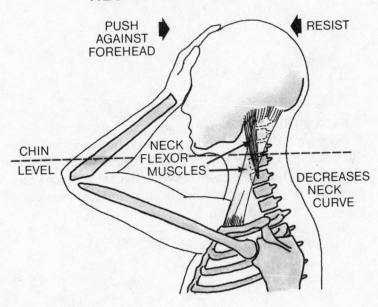

NECK STRENGTHENING 1

PUSH AGAINST FOREHEAD   →   ← RESIST

CHIN LEVEL

NECK FLEXOR MUSCLES

DECREASES NECK CURVE

6. NECK STRENGTHENING 2

1. Place your right hand on the right side of your forehead. **2.** Attempt to turn your head to the right. Resist with pressure from your hand. **3.** Hold for a count of five. **4.** Repeat. **5.** Place your left hand on the left side of your forehead and repeat the exercise.

NECK STRENGTHENING 2

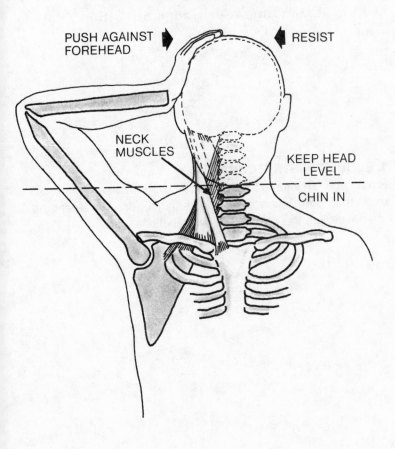

PUSH AGAINST
FOREHEAD

RESIST

NECK
MUSCLES

KEEP HEAD
LEVEL

CHIN IN

Extending Your Range of Motion

1. SHOULDER STRETCH

Rotate your shoulders in four precise movements—first up, then back, then down, then forward. Throughout the movement, hold the head high, the chin in. Do five repetitions.

SHOULDER STRETCH

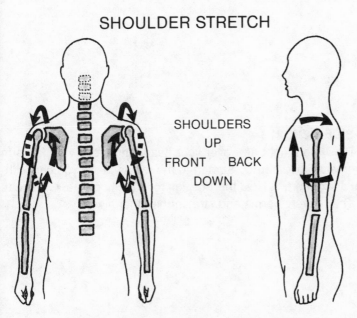

SHOULDERS
UP
FRONT   BACK
DOWN

WITH OR WITHOUT WEIGHTS IN HANDS

2. SIDE BENDING 1

1. Raise your right arm over your head, and cross your left arm over your abdomen. **2.** Stretch to the left as far as you can without discomfort. **3.** Hold this position for a count of five. **4.** Repeat. **5.** Then reverse arms and stretch the other side.

SIDE BENDING 1

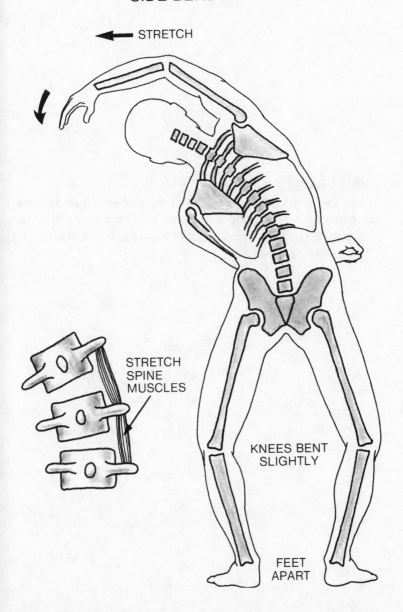

STRETCH

STRETCH
SPINE
MUSCLES

KNEES BENT
SLIGHTLY

FEET
APART

3. SIDE BENDING 2

1. With the feet together and away from the wall, lean into the wall with your arm straight. **2.** Push firmly on the pelvis with the other arm. **3.** Hold for a slow count of five. Release. **4.** Repeat. **5.** Then stretch the other side.

SIDE BENDING 2

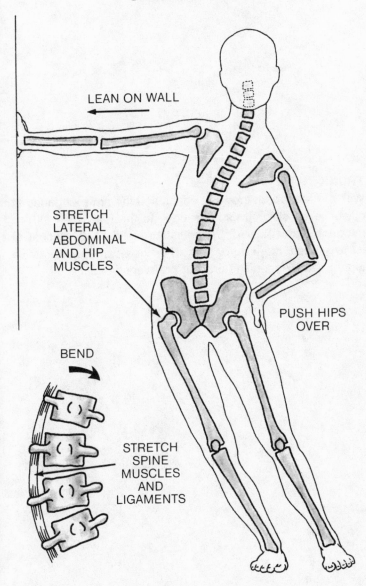

LEAN ON WALL

STRETCH
LATERAL
ABDOMINAL
AND HIP
MUSCLES

PUSH HIPS
OVER

BEND

STRETCH
SPINE
MUSCLES
AND
LIGAMENTS

4. TRUNK TWIST

1. With the feet apart, the knees bent, and the arms extended at shoulder level, slowly twist your body to the left as far as you comfortably can. **2.** Hold, then twist to the right. **3.** Repeat at least five times, more if you can. The head can turn or remain straight ahead, depending on your preference.

TRUNK TWIST

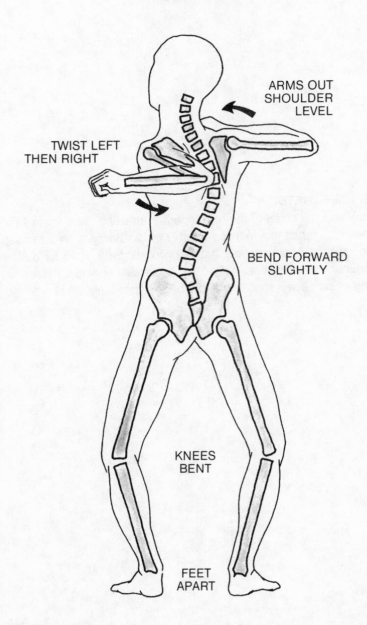

ARMS OUT
SHOULDER
LEVEL

TWIST LEFT
THEN RIGHT

BEND FORWARD
SLIGHTLY

KNEES
BENT

FEET
APART

5. HIP STRETCH 1

1. Place the soles of the feet together, drawing them toward the pelvis as far as they will comfortably go. **2.** Slowly push the knees toward the floor with your hands or forearms. **3.** Hold for a slow count of ten. Release. **4.** Repeat. **5.** Gently bending forward during exercise will stretch the low back beneficially.

HIP STRETCH 1

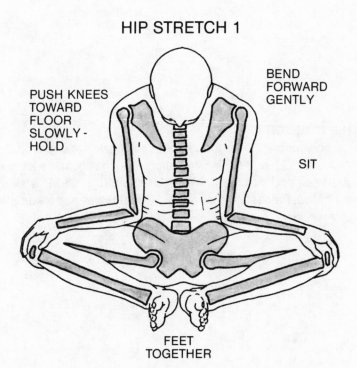

BEND
FORWARD
GENTLY

PUSH KNEES
TOWARD
FLOOR
SLOWLY -
HOLD

SIT

FEET
TOGETHER

6. HIP STRETCH 2

1. Lie on your back, with the low back flat against the ground. **2.** With one leg extended, bring the other leg to the chest, bending it at the knee and holding it under the knee. **3.** Hold for a slow count of five. Release. **4.** Repeat. **5.** Repeat the exercise with the legs reversed.

HIP STRETCH 2

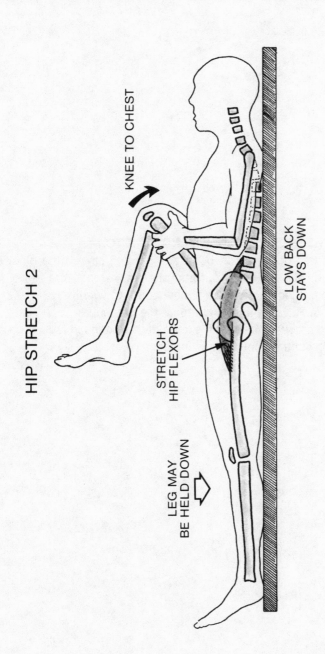

KNEE TO CHEST

STRETCH
HIP FLEXORS

LEG MAY
BE HELD DOWN

LOW BACK
STAYS DOWN

7. "PROTECTIVE" HAMSTRING STRETCH

1. Seated on the floor, bend one leg and stretch the other leg straight out. **2.** Reach out and attempt to touch the toe of the extended leg. **3.** Hold for a slow count of twenty. Relax. **4.** Repeat. **5.** Reverse legs and repeat the procedure.

Remember: Stiffening the knee of the extended leg will enable you to stretch another few degrees.

"PROTECTIVE" HAMSTRING STRETCH

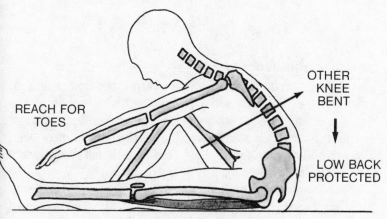

REACH FOR
TOES

OTHER
KNEE
BENT

LOW BACK
PROTECTED

HAMSTRING MUSCLES
STRETCH SLOWLY -
HOLD

8. HEEL CORD STRETCH

First movement: **1.** Place both feet several feet from a wall. **2.** Lean into the wall, supporting yourself with your hands on the wall at shoulder level. **3.** Bring one leg forward, bending the knee. **4.** With the other leg straight and the foot flat on the floor, lean forward, pressing the forward knee toward the wall until you feel a good stretch. **5.** Hold for a slow count of twenty.

Second movement: **1.** Bring the forward foot back alongside the rear foot, and hold it just off the ground. **2.** Move up and down slowly five times on the ball of the planted foot. **3.** Reverse feet and repeat both movements.

HEEL CORD STRETCH

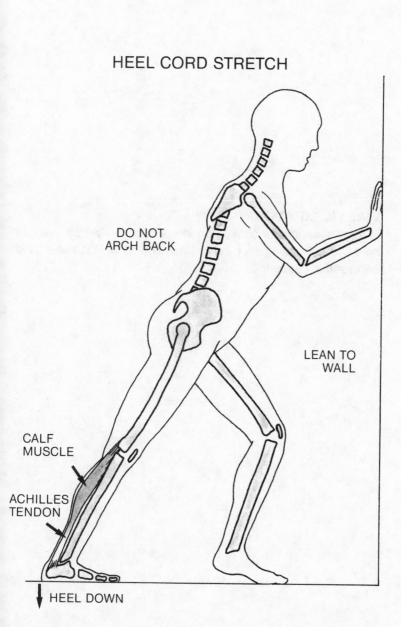

DO NOT
ARCH BACK

LEAN TO
WALL

CALF
MUSCLE

ACHILLES
TENDON

HEEL DOWN

9. PELVIC ROTATION

Sit straight up in your chair, then slowly and gently arch and curl the spine by rotating your pelvis back and forth. Rock back and forth for thirty seconds.

THE ONE-MINUTE BREAK:
PELVIC ROTATION

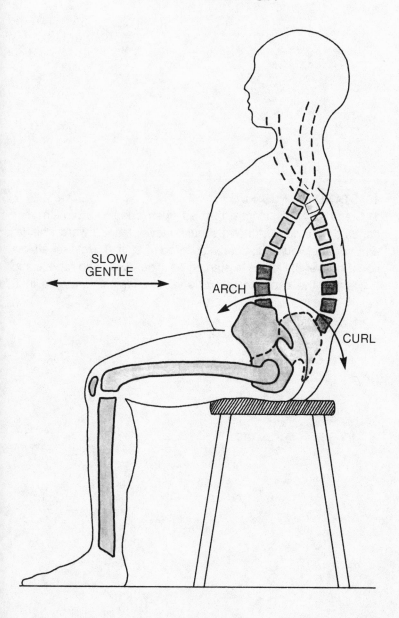

SLOW
GENTLE

ARCH

CURL

10. STANDING PUSH-UP

1. Stand at arm's length from an open doorway. **2.** With your hands on the door frame at shoulder level, lean forward, chin in, until you feel your chest getting a good stretch. **3.** Hold for a slow count of five. **4.** Return to starting position. **5.** Do two repetitions. **6.** Repeat the exercise raising and lowering the arms as indicated.

THE ONE-MINUTE BREAK:
STANDING PUSH-UP

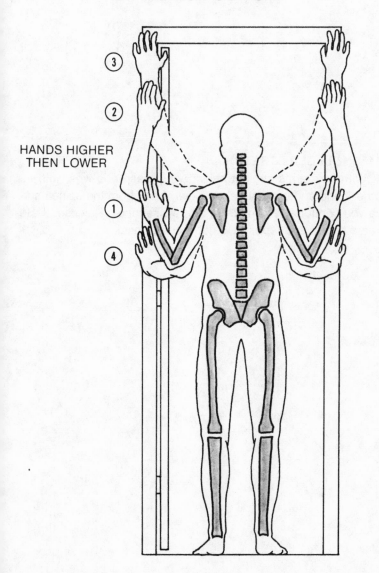

11. SHOULDER STRETCH 1

1. With your arms straight behind you, grasp one wrist with the other hand and pull both arms slowly back from the spine as far as you comfortably can. **2.** Hold a few seconds. Release. **3.** Reverse hands and repeat. Do not arch the neck.

THE ONE-MINUTE BREAK: SHOULDER STRETCH 1

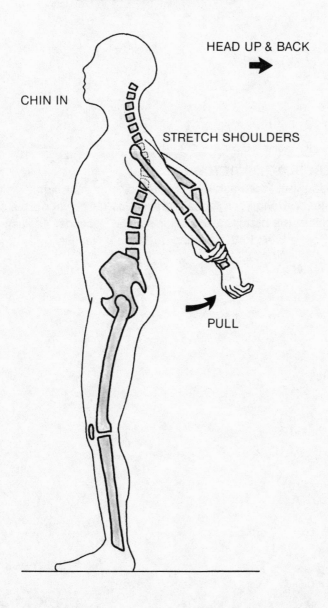

HEAD UP & BACK

CHIN IN

STRETCH SHOULDERS

PULL

12. SHOULDER STRETCH 2

1. Stand with your back to a counter, placing your hands on the counter. **2.** Bend your knees, dropping as far as your arms and shoulders will permit. **3.** Hold for several seconds. **4.** Push up until you're back to the starting position. **5.** Repeat.

THE ONE-MINUTE BREAK:
SHOULDER STRETCH 2

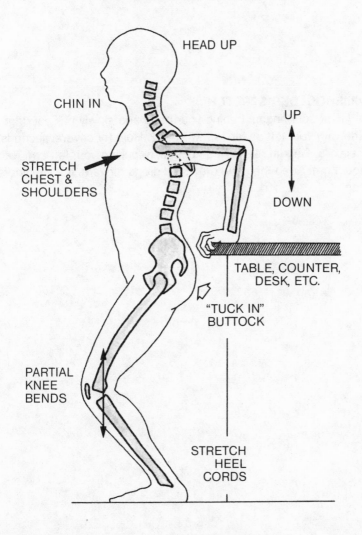

HEAD UP

CHIN IN

UP

DOWN

STRETCH
CHEST &
SHOULDERS

TABLE, COUNTER,
DESK, ETC.

"TUCK IN"
BUTTOCK

PARTIAL
KNEE
BENDS

STRETCH
HEEL
CORDS

13. SHOULDER STRETCH 3

1. Hook your fingers behind your head and slowly pull your right arm with your left as far as it will go. **2.** Hold for several seconds. Relax. **3.** Repeat. **4.** Reverse direction, pulling your left arm with your right. Keep the head erect. If it drops forward, the shoulders can't be stretched.

THE ONE-MINUTE BREAK:
SHOULDER STRETCH 3

HOOK HANDS BEHIND HEAD

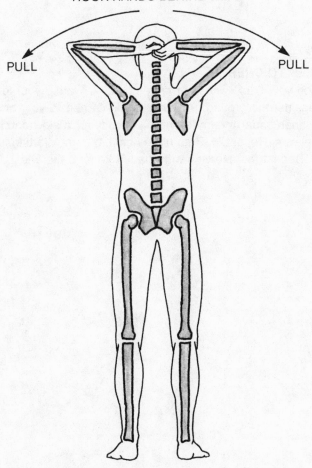

PULL

PULL

Defending Your Back

1. KNEES TO CHEST 1

1. Lie on your back, with your knees bent. **2.** Flatten your lower back against the ground. **3.** Bring the right knee to your chest, clasp hands under the knee and pull gently for a slow count of five. Relax. **4.** Repeat. **5.** Return the right leg to the starting position. **6.** Repeat the exercise with the left knee to the chest.

KNEES TO CHEST 1

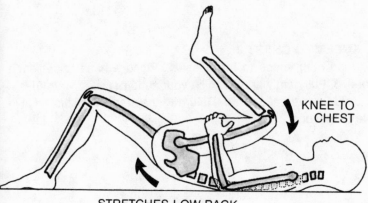

KNEE TO
CHEST

STRETCHES LOW BACK

2. KNEES TO CHEST 2

1. Bring both knees to the chest. **2.** Place a hand under each knee. **3.** Pull gently and try to lift your head between your knees. **4.** Hold for five seconds. **5.** Return to the starting position. **6.** Do five repetitions.

KNEES TO CHEST 2

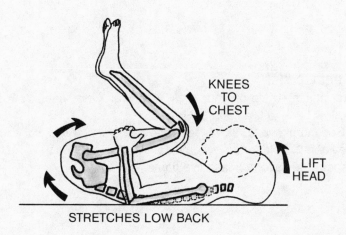

KNEES
TO
CHEST

LIFT
HEAD

STRETCHES LOW BACK

3. PELVIC TILT

First phase: **1.** Lie on your back, with your knees bent. **2.** Push the low back to the floor. **3.** Hold.

    Second phase: **1.** Slowly raise the pelvis one or two inches off the floor. **2.** Hold for a slow count of five. **3.** Return to the floor. **4.** Repeat the second phase five times.

"PELVIC TILT"

FIRST PHASE

② KNEES BENT   ① LIE ON BACK

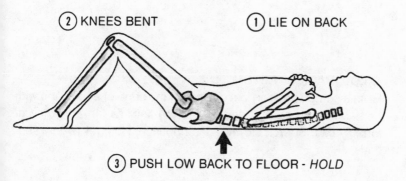

③ PUSH LOW BACK TO FLOOR - *HOLD*

SECOND PHASE

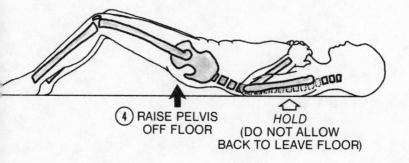

④ RAISE PELVIS   *HOLD*
   OFF FLOOR   (DO NOT ALLOW
         BACK TO LEAVE FLOOR)

4. LOW BACK STRETCH

From a seated position in a chair or at the edge of a bed, and with feet and knees apart, bend toward the floor as far as you comfortably can. Stretch slowly—don't bounce. Hold for twenty seconds.

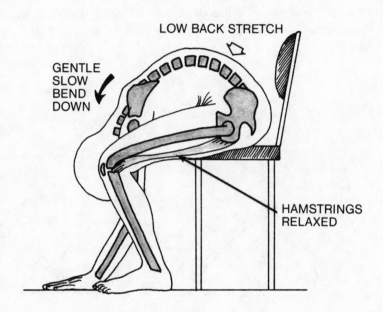

LOW BACK STRETCH

GENTLE
SLOW
BEND
DOWN

HAMSTRINGS
RELAXED

5. SIT-UPS

There are five stages to this exercise. Perform at whatever level is comfortable for you, advancing to the next stage when you can.

SIT-UP: STAGE 1

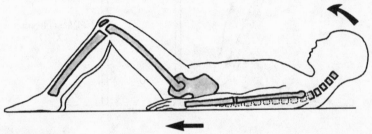

Stage One:

1. Begin the exercise lying on the floor, with your arms at your sides and your knees bent. **2.** Lift your head from the floor as far as you comfortably can. At the same time, slide your hands toward your feet. **3.** Hold for a slow count of five. **4.** Return to the starting position. Relax. Do as many repetitions as you can until mildly fatigued.

SIT-UP: STAGE 2

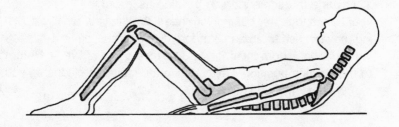

Stage Two:
1. Assume the same starting position as in Stage One. **2.** This time, slowly lift your head and your shoulders as high as you comfortably can. At the same time, slide your hands along the floor toward your feet. **3.** Hold for a slow count of five. **4.** Return to starting position. Relax. Do as many repetitions as you comfortably can until mildly fatigued.

Stage Three:

1. Assume the same starting position as in Stage One. 2. "Peel" your back off the floor by raising the vertebrae in stages, to approximately forty-five degrees. As you do, keep the arms forward and parallel to the ground. 3. Hold for a count of five. 4. Return to the starting position. Relax. 5. Do as many repetitions as you comfortably can until mildly fatigued.

Stage Four:

1. Assume the same starting position as in Stage One, but lace your hands together behind your head. 2. With your elbows pointing forward, rise to an angle of forty-five degrees, again by "peeling" your back from the floor. 3. Hold for a count of five. 4. Return to the starting position. Relax. 5. Do as many repetitions as you can until mildly fatigued.

Stage Five:

1. Assume the same starting position as in Stage Four, but pull your elbows back as far as they will go. 2. Rise to an angle of forty-five degrees, again by "peeling" your back from the floor. 3. Hold for a count of five. 4. Return to the starting position. Relax. 5. Do as many repetitions as you can until mildly fatigued.

SIT-UPS: STAGES 3, 4 & 5

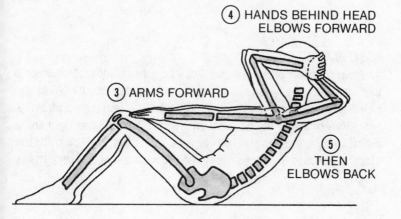

④ HANDS BEHIND HEAD
ELBOWS FORWARD

③ ARMS FORWARD

⑤
THEN
ELBOWS BACK

6. SIT-BACK

1. Wrap the feet around a post, or hook them under a chair or a bed. **2.** With the knees well bent, the hands laced behind the head, and the elbows out, lean back until you feel a mild strain. **3.** Hold this position for a count of five. **4.** Turn to the right for a count of five, then to the left for a count of five. **5.** Return to the starting position. **6.** Do as many repetitions as you can until mildly fatigued.

ISOMETRIC SIT-BACK
STAGE 1

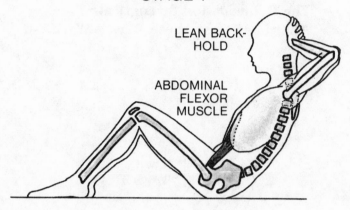

LEAN BACK-
HOLD

ABDOMINAL
FLEXOR
MUSCLE

ISOMETRIC SIT-BACK
STAGE 2

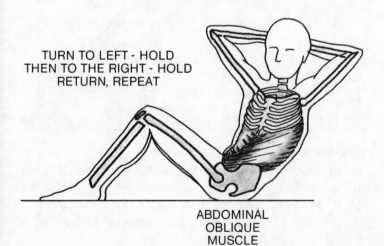

TURN TO LEFT - HOLD
THEN TO THE RIGHT - HOLD
RETURN, REPEAT

ABDOMINAL
OBLIQUE
MUSCLE

The Rejuvenation Strength Routine
Alternate Days, Three Days a Week

PUSHUPS

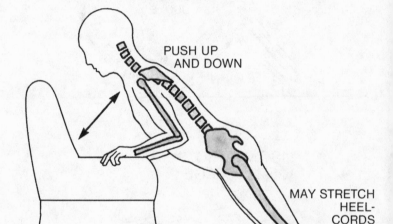

PUSH UP
AND DOWN

MAY STRETCH
HEEL-
CORDS

1. PUSH-UPS

1. Brace your arms at shoulder height, either against a door frame, a countertop, a chair, or the floor, depending on your condition. **2.** Bend at the elbows, letting your body drop forward as far as you can. **3.** Push up until your elbows are straight. **4.** Repeat until mildly fatigued.

2. DIPS

1. With your feet on the floor, place your hands, palms down, on the arms or seat of a chair. **2.** Stretch your legs in front of you. **3.** Lower your body as far as you can, while bending the arms. **4.** Return to the starting position. **5.** Do as many repetitions as you can until mildly fatigued. To increase difficulty, place the feet on a coffee table or a chair, or on the edge of your bed.

DIPS

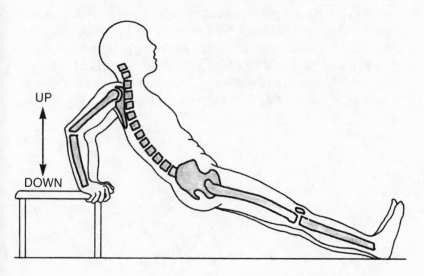

UP

DOWN

3. HALF SQUATS

1. Put your back against a smooth door, a refrigerator, or a secure wall mirror. **2.** Place your feet a few inches away from the surface. **3.** Flatten your low back against the surface. **4.** Slide down the surface until your legs are bent at an angle of forty-five degrees. **5.** Return to the starting position. **6.** Do as many repetitions as you can until mildly fatigued.

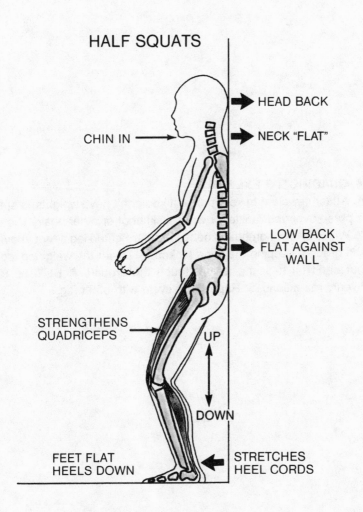

HALF SQUATS

HEAD BACK

NECK "FLAT"

CHIN IN

LOW BACK
FLAT AGAINST
WALL

STRENGTHENS
QUADRICEPS

UP

DOWN

FEET FLAT
HEELS DOWN

STRETCHES
HEEL CORDS

4. QUADRICEPS EXERCISE

1. Attach a weight to your ankle. If you don't have weights, drape a purse over your ankle, or wear a ski boot or other heavy shoe. **2.** With the unweighted leg bent, lift the weighted leg a foot above the ground, keeping the knee locked. **3.** Lower the weighted leg, but don't let it or the weight touch the ground. **4.** Build up to twenty repetitions. **5.** Repeat the cycle with other leg.

QUADRICEPS EXERCISE

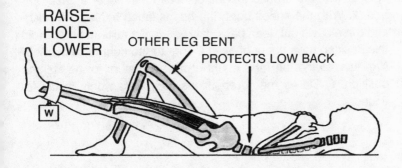

RAISE-
HOLD-
LOWER

OTHER LEG BENT

PROTECTS LOW BACK

W

5. SIT-BACK

(Skip if you've done it earlier in the back-strengthening routine.)
1. Wrap the feet around a post, or hook them under a chair or a bed. **2.** With the knees bent, the hands laced behind the head, and the elbows out, lean back until you feel a mild strain. **3.** Hold this position for a count of five. **4.** Turn to the right for a count of five, then to the left for a count of five. **5.** Return to the starting position. **6.** Do as many repetitions as you can until mildly fatigued.

ISOMETRIC SIT-BACK
STAGE 1

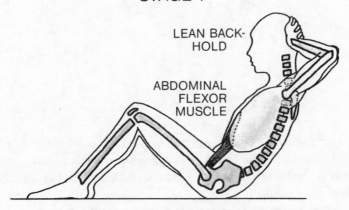

LEAN BACK-
HOLD

ABDOMINAL
FLEXOR
MUSCLE

ISOMETRIC SIT-BACK
STAGE 2

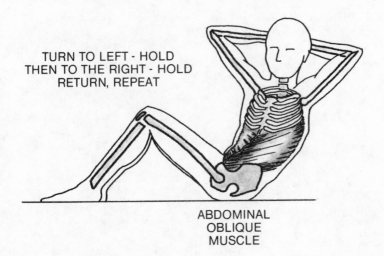

TURN TO LEFT - HOLD
THEN TO THE RIGHT - HOLD
RETURN, REPEAT

ABDOMINAL
OBLIQUE
MUSCLE

The Rejuventation Walk—Daily

Walk rapidly for at least twenty minutes a day, but preferably for an hour. If you can't walk every day, try to walk at least three days a week—the days on which you don't do your Rejuvenation Strength Routine.

Walk shorter distances at a faster pace in preference to longer distances at a slower pace.

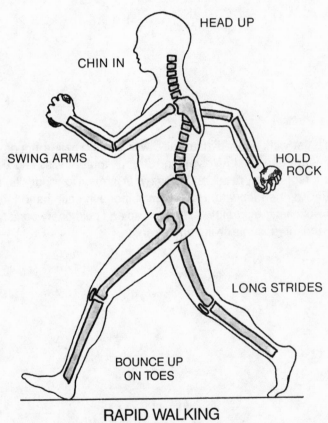

HEAD UP

CHIN IN

SWING ARMS

HOLD
ROCK

LONG STRIDES

BOUNCE UP
ON TOES

RAPID WALKING
THE BEST EXERCISE OF ALL

Don't just walk. Walk dynamically, with a rapid gait, a bounce to your step, and total involvement of your torso. Twist and bend your torso; swing, raise, and cross your arms. Do windmills, first backward, then forward. Hold a small stone in each hand to add to the challenge, promote extra cardiac and pulmonary conditioning, and increase flexibility and strength.

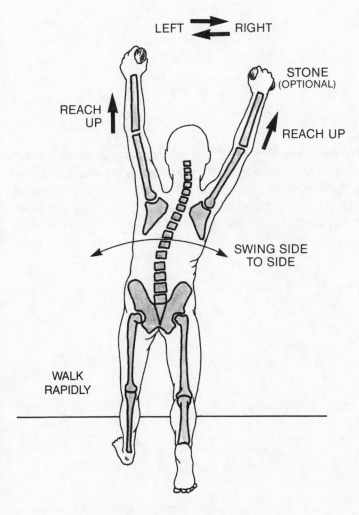

LEFT RIGHT

STONE
(OPTIONAL)

REACH
UP

REACH UP

SWING SIDE
TO SIDE

WALK
RAPIDLY

WALKING-PLUS

Belly Breathing: Figure 1 shows the normal position of the chest and abdomen. In Figure 2, the abdomen is extended, which lets the diaphragm fall, thus creating more room for air in the chest, which expands to larger than normal size (Figure 3). Belly breathing may be done standing, sitting or prone.

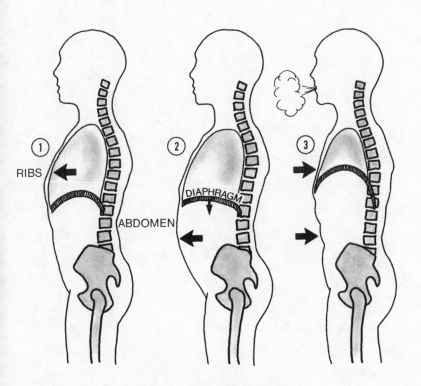

RIBS

DIAPHRAGM

ABDOMEN

BELLY BREATHING

1. INHALE. RIBS EXPAND.

2. CONTINUE INHALE. ABDOMEN EXPANDS.

3. EXHALE. BOTH CONTRACT.

PART THREE

MAINTAINING A YOUTHFUL LIFE

12. RELAXATION: A MUST

Reversing the effects of aging is not just a matter of rejuvenating prematurely aged tissue with a well-aimed series of exercises. To be successful, the program must encompass four other important components of a youthful life: relaxation, nutrition, health, and mental attitude.

Let's look at them in that order.

It's Time to Relax

We can do things a thousand times a day with never any problem, but doing the same things when we're emotionally upset can result in serious injury. A ten-pound bag of grapefruit can throw Sally Jones's back out if she happens to be thinking about how angry she is at her husband as she puts her groceries into the car. It's tension that will be her undoing.

Tension is an ominous thing, as virulent as a bacteria, a virus, or a cancer. Not only can it do bodily harm, it can aggravate diseases—even cause them. It can produce changes in the blood vessels, the gastrointestinal system, and the body's tissues. A brain distracted by anger or anxiety can be rendered incapable of coordinating the complex series of movements required for Sally Jones to get her groceries safely stowed in her car.

Tension can rob muscles of their ability to function. Worse yet, tension can cause muscles to deteriorate.

There is only one thing that can immunize you against the insidious effect of tension, and that is relaxation.

Most Americans never learn how to relax. That's a pity, because quite apart from its emotional benefits, a period of relaxation is absolutely essential for anyone interested in reversing the physiological clock.

The tissues in our muscles must rest in order to recover from the acute trauma of everyday life. If we don't have the ability to relax, these tissues never completely recover. Each day, we develop a little more microscopic damage; when enough damage has accumulated we get degenerative change.

Now let's take a closer look at exactly what happens physiologically to a body operating under the constraints of tension.

Tension: Its Effect on Muscles

To get a feeling for what happens in your body when you are tense, try this little exercise. Seat yourself in front of a friend and shout as angrily and convincingly as possible, "No, no, no, no, no. . . ." Continue for a full minute. Then switch your mood, and in an inviting voice, say—meaning it—"Yes, yes, yes, yes, yes. . . ." for another minute. You should feel an enormous difference throughout your body between the two situations. When you are being combative, you will notice a hardening of your face and neck, and perhaps a tightness in your chest and a tingling in your limbs. During the receptive phase of the exercise, you will probably experience a feeling of fluidity and ease.

When we are tense—as we are when we're angry—we are causing every muscle in our body to work, to contract strongly. Because they are working so hard, our muscles are using oxygen at an accelerated rate. Oxygen is the chemical agent that gives our muscles energy; as an engine needs fuel, they need oxygen to perform. But we're not giving them the oxygen they need. We can't because at the same time that we're working our muscles, their contraction is squeezing off the blood vessels that would bring oxygen-laden blood to them. Our muscles now are forced to feed on the limited reserves within them.

If the situation remains unchanged—as it often does when ongoing tension causes constant muscle contraction—our muscles' supply of oxygen will soon be depleted.

Oxygen depletion has the same effect on our bodies as fuel starvation has on a motor. When a motor does not get enough fuel, it runs poorly. When the fuel stops altogether, the engine dies.

When we don't get enough oxygen, our bodies don't perform efficiently. Without oxygen, we're dead.

Tension: Its Effect on Movement

Some years ago the *Journal of the American Medical Association* reported on the results of an investigation of back problems among seasoned workers at a Ford assembly plant in Detroit. The researcher, a clinical psychologist, first noted that the men who had suffered the injuries were unlikely accident victims. Not only were they experienced workers, they were strong and in excellent health. They were completely capable of handling the tasks required of them. Nor were their work loads excessive either in terms of the amount of weight lifted or the time spent on lifting tasks. Accordingly, the psychologist ruled out all physical reasons for the injuries.

Then he interviewed the injured workers about their emotional states at the time of their accidents. He found that in every single case the injury occurred when the worker was angry, or depressed, or under some form of nervous tension.

Nervous tension causes us to misuse our bodies. When the computer in our brain that normally makes our muscles work in a proper coordinated manner is momentarily disrupted, we stress and strain our bodies. Almost inevitably we damage them.

When we stand, bend, stoop or squat to pick something up, our spines strengthen and lengthen. When all is well, every muscle elongates at the right time, at the right speed, and in the right sequence and—like a plant swaying in the breeze—the spine bends smoothly, its vertebrae performing in an exquisitely coordinated manner. Our backs are like a symphony—until we become tense and anxious.

When we're tense, the movement of the vertebrae is no longer synchronized. The muscles that control them twist. They don't let go at the right time. In the old expression, they zig when they should have zagged.

As an angry woman with ten pounds of grapefruit will surely discover, bending over without releasing the muscles that allow your back to bend is like driving a car without taking your brakes off. A breakdown is inevitable.

Relaxation: When, and How

Relaxation is the only way to reestablish a balance between the oxygen input and the oxygen expenditure in our muscles. It's the only way to release the nervous tension that we carry around with us—tension that prematurely ages our tissues. The question is not whether we need to relax, it's when and how to do it.

When? There is no such thing as an ideal time for relaxing. It's a matter of individual preference and schedules. I know an attorney who can't work effectively in the afternoon unless he takes an hour at noon to run around a nearby track. I know others who take a Jacuzzi each evening when they return home from work. My own preference is for two periods each day, early morning and after work. As I've indicated, I'm an early riser; by five-thirty each morning, I'm walking in the coastal foothills adjacent to my home, feeling the sea breeze on my skin, smelling the freshness of the earth and plants, watching for rabbits and deer, listening to the birds. It's an exquisite time, well worth the extra hour of sleep I trade for it.

When I return home at the end of the day, I immediately take off my shoes and go barefoot in the house. It's my way of breaking my ties with civilization. I'm fortunate in that I live in Southern California and have a swimming pool. On most evenings, I go for a long swim before dinner. That's my way to wipe out the cares of the day, and get rid of debilitating tension.

There ought to be at least one and preferably two periods set aside for relaxation—precisely when is completely up to you. In addition, there should be moments during the day when, feeling the tension that's built up inside you, you break off whatever you're doing and spend a minute or two in some manner that helps you relax. Whenever I feel the tension mounting, I get up from my desk and stretch my muscles. My patients are sometimes startled to see me put a foot on my desk and lean over my leg to stretch my calf and hamstrings.

In Chapter 7, we discussed the "One-Minute Break," five exercises done several times during the working day, preferably every hour, to maintain flexibility in the chest and shoulders, and improve posture. That break, performed religiously, will do wonders to diminish tension and its ravages.

Now, *how* to relax during a special period each day?

Exercise is a form of relaxation. It's something you should do at least three times a week, even better, five times a week and ideally every day. If you're exercising daily, your tissues may be getting all the relaxation they need, particularly if your bouts of exercise follow your period of maximum tension.

Because you're working during exercise, it may be difficult for you to accept intellectually that you're also relaxing in the process, but in most cases, particularly during mild exercise, it happens to be true. In competitive sports, players afflicted with a great deal of tension aren't getting much relaxation, but that problem is almost never present during bouts of walking and stretching.

When you exercise, you first contract and then relax the muscles. You *must* relax the muscle in order to contract it again. In addition to its contract-and-relax cycle, exercise produces tranquilizing chemicals called endorphins, which are both pain killers and relaxants. Finally, exercise produces an electrical effect on the neurological connections in the muscles, which causes them to relax. So in the process of exercising mildly (short of stress), we are relaxing—through mechanical, chemical, and electrical reactions.

When you take a chemical designed to relax you, it must pass through the bloodstream to produce an effect, a process that can take many minutes and conceivably an hour. Mild exercise functions in the same way as a pill, but in a far healthier manner. It's not a pill chemically made in a laboratory; it's a drug made by the body. The pill may have side effects; exercise, performed correctly, has none.

Stretching is the best kind of exercise for relaxation. If you did nothing more than perform all the stretching exercises described in this book, you'd have an excellent relaxation program right there.

A daily, or almost daily, fitness walk of at least twenty minutes would provide another healthy break in the day.

In addition to stretching and walking, I recommend a third form of relaxation, a special breathing technique that puts extra amounts of oxygen into your blood at the same time it puts you into a mild, safe, and thoroughly enjoyable trance.

The "Belly Breathing" Trance

To understand what follows, let's discuss one final bit of anatomy:

The amount of oxygen you take into your body with each breath depends on how large a breath you take. The size of the breath you take, in turn, depends, basically, on two factors: the capacity of your lungs, and the position of your diaphragm. Let's recall, one more time, the importance of posture in maximizing your vital capacity, the amount of air you can take into your lungs. Rounded shoulders diminish the lungs' capacity; only when you're standing or sitting upright can the lungs function to their fullest. If your upper body is in an erect position, the only other variable is the position of your diaphragm.

The diaphragm is the partition that separates your chest cavity from your abdominal cavity. The position of the diaphragm is relative to the position of your abdominal wall, which we popularly refer to as the "belly." When the belly is in, the diaphragm remains in an up position; when the belly is out, the diaphragm moves down.

Learning to breathe with your belly has important physiological advantages. With the diaphragm in the down position, the lungs have additional room to expand. The volume of air they can handle increases by as much as 25 percent. This increase in air to the lungs gives you much greater endurance, and also pumps more oxygen to the blood.

Given these impressive advantages, one would think that we would all want to protrude our bellies as we take in a breath. Much as we may want to, we rarely do it—and the reason we don't is tension. Tension makes the stomach muscles stiffen; when they're taut, the belly can't expand. It takes a concentrated effort to relax the belly and make it protrude each time we take a breath —and that's where the relaxation effect comes in.

Meditation, the most popular of all relaxation techniques, essentially involves controlled, rhythmic breathing, and focusing on a word, an idea, or an action. Transcendental meditators use a "mantra," a word that they repeat with each breath. Other meditators repeat the word "one" over and over again, or something else simple, easy, requiring little thought. Still others create images in their minds and project themselves into them. One friend of ours, an educator, uses the image of a set of steep stairs that lead from a beautiful sandy cove in La Jolla, California, up to a magnificent house. In her mind she makes her way step by step either up or down that staircase. She has yet to reach the beach if she starts at the house, or the house if she starts at the beach.

Whatever technique is used, the result is self-hypnosis.

The thought of putting themselves into a trance is frightening to some people. In fact, there is absolutely nothing to fear. You have complete control of yourself going in, and you can come out of it at any time. The experience during the trance is one of peace and serenity; you can feel the tension ebbing away; your body goes soft; your limbs begin to tingle; all at once you feel yourself moving into a physical realm you have never been in before. Time does seem to stand still. The feeling is so delicious that you're almost sad when you decide to terminate it.

What we're going to do is use belly breathing as our focus in inducing this meditative trance.

The Belly Breathing Technique

STEP 1: Begin with a slow, deep breath, either through your nose or your mouth. As you inhale, extend the muscles of your abdomen.
STEP 2: Fill your lungs with air.
STEP 3: Let the air out of your lungs.
STEP 4: Draw in the muscles of the belly.

Although belly breathing is quickly learned, it will take a conscious effort at the onset—which is exactly what you want. It trains you to concentrate on what you're doing. As soon as you've mastered the technique, do your breathing with your eyes closed. At the beginning, however, you may want to place your hands on your belly and watch them to be sure you're breathing correctly. If your hands rise as you inhale, and fall as you exhale, you are. But even long after you've become proficient, and no longer need to use your hands, you should focus on the four-step breathing process. That focus will gradually reduce the clutter in

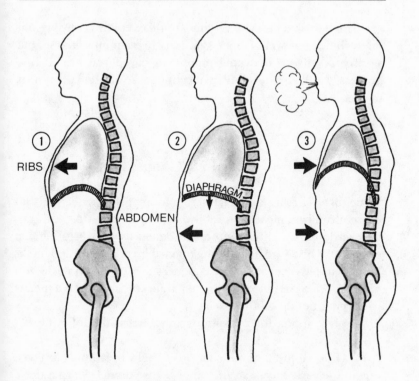

BELLY BREATHING

(1) INHALE. RIBS EXPAND.

(2) CONTINUE INHALE. ABDOMEN EXPANDS.

(3) EXHALE. BOTH CONTRACT.

your mind; your breathing will become increasingly deeper and more rhythmic; finally you'll feel yourself slipping into a state of suspension. If you lose your focus from time to time, don't let it bother you; everybody does. Just bring your mind back to your breathing, and your rising and falling belly. No matter whether your mind remains focused or wanders, that deep, rhythmic breathing is doing wonders for your body.

No matter what else you're doing to relax, try this belly breathing technique as well. Do it for at least five minutes at first, and work yourself up to twenty minutes a day if you can. In the process, you'll also develop an uncanny sense of when the time is up.

Don't Overdo a Good Thing

Some form of relaxation each day is as important as eating. Because it can become as enjoyable as eating, it can—like eating—be overdone. We all know the consequences of overeating; we should also be aware that getting hooked on relaxation and meditation can have negative consequences as well. It won't do you much good to pass through life in a trance; relaxation is a means to an end, not an end in itself.

My prescription for relaxation, therefore, is the following:

• Two 10-to-20-minute periods of belly breathing each day, one in the early morning, the other before dinner. During these periods, take the telephone off the hook, ask the family for quiet, and go to a room where you can shut the door and be alone.

• Frequent brief periods of relaxation throughout the day, in which you do the four exercises in the One-Minute Break, and take three or four deep breaths, using the belly breathing technique.

13. A REJUVENATING MENU

There is no question that a proper diet, like proper exercise, diminishes the ravages of aging, and there is some reason to believe that—again, like exercise—it might actually prolong life as well. The question is, what kind of diet?

I take the same position about the subject of diet, and the related question of weight, as I do about the subject of exercise. I find much popular advice misguided, and some of it dead wrong.

In more than forty years of medical practice, I have seen a plethora of gimmicks, promising instant health or weight loss. They don't work, first, because they take a fragmentary approach, and second, because they're unrealistic.

Recent studies have shown that fat deposited in the cells of people destined to be obese is there at birth, meaning that for some persons, excess weight is a hereditary problem and not one for which an individual should feel guilty. This doesn't mean, however, that the individual should ignore excess poundage. Far from it.

Reaching and maintaining an acceptable weight is critical to the process of growing and staying young. Not only do extra pounds place extra stress on joints, low back, hips, knees, and feet, they represent other very real health hazards as well. If you are 25 percent over your normal weight—for a medium-sized woman that's just thirty pounds—you are flirting with high blood pressure, arteriosclerosis (hardening of the arteries), heart attacks, strokes, diabetes, and medical problems beyond this list.

If you're overweight, you must be realistic about your problem and use realistic strategies to overcome it. That means learning to control your appetite as opposed to starving.

We diet to become and remain healthy, not to starve off weight. The body requires food as a machine requires fuel. Food not only supplies the body with energy, but helps rebuild tissue. As we age, our tissues become increasingly worn, and the need for specific nutrients to repair the damage becomes even greater. Yet these essential nutrients are often the very ones we sacrifice when we embark on crash diets. Result: Dieting can do your body more harm than good.

There *is* a healthy and simple way to lose excess pounds and maintain a desirable weight. The program boils down to five basic, comfortable, sensible rules.

The trouble with basic, comfortable, sensible rules is that they're not as alluring as gimmicks. They don't promise an immediate loss of twenty pounds the first week, and fifty pounds the first month. They don't tell you that calories don't count and that you can eat whatever you please. They don't suggest that the answer is to eat only one thing, be it lamb chops or grapefruit or ice cream, or to eat nothing but protein. On the other hand, the five basic rules are something a physician like myself can recommend knowing that permanent weight loss will result if you obey them, and that you won't get sick in the process.

Rule One: Eat All Kinds of Foods

A "well-balanced diet" is not a nutritionist's cliché. It does not require long lists of official or X-rated foods. It *is* the key to the rejuvenation of tissue.

When a cell metabolizes, it utilizes oxygen and burns off energy. The entire cell, however, does not get used in the process. A certain amount of "garbage" or waste is left over, something akin to the brown grease at the bottom of a pan when you've fried an egg. These free radicals, as the residue of metabolized cells are called, proceed to float through the body and attack other cells. The cells they damage become free radicals, in turn. Infections, injuries, and even X rays create still more free radicals, until vast numbers of these undesirables are visiting the body.

To remain healthy, the body must rid itself of these free radicals in an amount exactly equal to the number it creates. It does so naturally by excreting them. But to do that properly and regularly, it needs the assistance of vitamins and minerals provided by a well-balanced diet. Unfortunately, most fad diets eliminate essential nutrients such as starches and fats that are required for proper function.

I'm not suggesting that it's a good idea to pile your plate high with fettucini Alfredo. But in limited quantities as an occasional treat, it's not going to hurt, and the cheese and cream can be good for you. In spite of what the media has been pounding into us for all these years, we *need* a certain amount of fat to replace tissue loss and metabolize vitamins.

The secret to a healthy diet is not to cut out entire groups of food, but to cut *down* on the ones that are high in calories, fats, and cholesterol.

Your body has certain requirements if it is to remain healthy and function as it should. These include:

Protein. Without a doubt the best nutritional component, protein repairs tissues that are injured and replaces those that are lost. Fish and fowl are the purest forms of protein, especially when broiled without butter or oil. Often forgotten, cooked dried beans and peas are also excellent sources of protein, and inexpensive as well.

Recent evidence suggests that fish and fish oil in the diet can reduce the risk of heart attacks. Dutch researchers who studied hundreds of middle-aged men for twenty years reported that those who ate no fish were more than twice as likely to die of a heart attack as those who ate fish every day. Even those subjects who ate fish only once or twice a week appeared more resistant to heart disease. In another study, researchers at the Oregon Health

Sciences University in Portland found that a diet rich in fish oil was more effective in reducing fat and cholesterol in the blood than a diet rich in vegetable oils, such as safflower and corn oil.

Vitamins. If we all ate enough fruits and vegetables, vitamin companies would be put out of business. "Enough" means at least two and preferably three servings of green and yellow vegetables each day (serve cooked vegetables al dente, with lemon juice rather than butter; a little oil in salad dressings won't hurt); at least one serving of fresh fruit (citrus fruit is an excellent source of vitamin C); and a generous serving of grains such as oats and wheat germ (a source of vitamin E, which has been credited with slowing down the effects of aging, as well as vitamins B and D).

Minerals. A critical part of any healthy diet, minerals help build body tissues and regulate body functions. As we get older, two minerals in particular, calcium and potassium, play an increasingly important role in our diets. Dairy products and leafy green vegetables are an excellent source of calcium, which helps prevent osteoporosis, a weakening of the bones (more about that in the next chapter). Older patients on salt-free diets or who are using diuretics should be sure they're getting enough potassium by eating plenty of green vegetables, bananas, and citrus fruits.

Fiber. Although fiber has no nutritional value, it serves two important functions. First, it benefits bowel function, which is critical to the elimination of those dangerous free radicals in our systems. Second, it helps control weight, replacing foods that have higher caloric content and satisfying hunger by causing the satiety mechanism (the one that tells you you're full) to function. Third, fiber in diet binds with fat. It literally combines with fat globules and prevents or decreases fat storage. This may be the most valuable benefit of high fiber in the diet.

Fiber is found in complex carbohydrate foods—grains, fruits, and most vegetables. High-fiber foods include potatoes (contrary to popular belief, they're not fattening if eaten without butter or sour cream and are full of vitamins as well as fiber); cooked dried peas and beans; whole grain breads and cereals; fresh fruits; and raw vegetables, particularly celery, carrots, and broccoli.

Whereas simple sugars are fattening, complex carbohydrates —which are also sugars—are nutritious and nonfattening. They may also be weight-reducing, in that they prevent fat storage at the same time they supply energy. Ingesting complex carbohydrates increases the metabolic rate—the rate of burning calories —five to eight times over the increase produced by the ingestion of calories that supply little or no nutrition.

Each meal you take should include two or more servings of complex carbohydrates. Overall, complex carbohydrates should constitute 80 percent of your intake. Together with proper exercise, that amount of complex carbohydrates will initiate and maintain weight loss and still supply good nutrition. No one who eats two portions of grain, vegetables, or fruit at each meal will ever feel deprived.

Rule Two: Minimize Certain Foods

Eating all kinds of foods doesn't mean eating everything all the time. There are specific foods that you want to go easy on. Those with:

Cholesterol and saturated fats. While it's true that you need some fat in your diet, too much of the wrong kind can lead to heart disease, breast cancer, colon and prostate cancer, and hardening of the arteries. Though most people think they don't have to worry about arteriosclerosis until they reach fifty, the problem can begin to develop when we're children. Controlling—minimizing, not eliminating—the amount of fat we consume and opting for unsaturated fats such as vegetable oil in cooking instead of saturated fats such as butter will help minimize a condition that may have begun years before.

Sugar. It takes sixty-nine minutes of very brisk walking to burn up the calories contained in one slice of apple pie. Low in nutrients and high in calories, sugars and sweets not only contribute to weight gain and tooth decay, but also upset the balance of fat and protein in the body.

Cakes, pies, cookies, and ice cream are obvious sources of sugar. Others are less obvious; if you don't read the labels on the bottles or cans you select at the supermarket, you won't know how much sugar you're ingesting. Stay away from products that list the following as a principal ingredient (such ingredients are usually the first ones mentioned): sugar, sucrose, honey, corn syrup, corn sweeteners, molasses, dextrose, fructose, glucose, maltose, or brown sugar.

I'm not suggesting that all sugar be eliminated from the diet. Doing that might impair the function of an important chemical in the brain called "serotonin," which helps control the appetite. When we eat sweets, the brain normally responds by releasing increased amounts of serotonin, which has the effect of satisfying hunger. Eliminating all sugars from the diet, therefore, could be counterproductive. The best possible way to consume sugar is in the form of complex carbohydrates.

Sodium. A mineral that's most commonly found in table salt, sodium in excessive quantities can lead to high blood pressure, fluid retention, and heart disease. Use salt sparingly in cooking and at the table. Remember that bouillon cubes, soy sauce, steak sauce, and barbecue sauce all contain high levels of salt. Eat sparingly of cured or smoked meats or fish: ham, bacon, sausages, hot dogs, luncheon meats, lox, herring, and sardines. Go easy on salted crackers, pretzels, and potato chips and on pickled foods. Again, read labels; avoid products with high levels of salt, sodium, and monosodium glutamate (MSG). Be aware that most convenience foods such as canned or instant soup (some of the best-known brands carry MSG), cake mixes, and frozen dinners contain added salt and sodium.

Rule Three: Eat What You Need,
Not What You Want

Since food serves to fuel the body, how much fuel you need directly relates to what you're asking your body to do. The construction worker who carries heavy building materials throughout the day and the ski racer in training may require as much as three thousand calories a day. A certified public accountant, on the other hand, would probably do very well with two thousand calories or even less, since his workday does not require as much physical output of energy. (Mental output may be exhausting, but it just doesn't burn calories.) If that same accountant went on a backpacking trip, however, he would need more calories to sustain him.

Activity level, however, is not the only factor in determining how many calories we should consume. We all know and envy that one person who seems to eat everything in sight and never gain a pound. The reason he or she can get away with it and the rest of us can't is because metabolic rates differ. There are certain people who can absorb, utilize, and benefit from more calories than others. Unfortunately, most of us don't fall into that category. We must moderate our intake or suffer the consequences.

It would be great if we could always count on our bodies to tell us when to stop eating. It's actually supposed to work that way. At a certain point, the satiety mechanism, which is akin to software in the central nervous system, is supposed to notify the brain that enough food has been consumed. But that mechanism doesn't always function properly, and scientists are still trying to understand why. Eventually, the day may come when doctors will be able to monitor and control satiety with pills, shots, or mechanical treatments. For the moment, however, we have to rely on ourselves.

Two tricks should help. One: Place on your plate the amount of food you've determined you need, and then avoid all second helpings no matter how good the food is. Two: Eat slowly and chew, chew, chew. You'll find that even a small meal satisfies the appetite when eaten at a leisurely pace. Remember: Prolonged chewing prolongs the pleasure.

Rule Four: Don't Skip Meals

It's difficult to monitor the quantity of food you consume under the best of circumstances; skip a meal and putting your fork down the next time you eat becomes nearly impossible. The voracious appetite you bring to the table all but guarantees that you'll misjudge the amount of food you need. Result: You put away more calories in that one sitting than you "saved" by not eating breakfast or lunch.

To make sure that you don't get carried away, eat three satisfying, low-calorie meals at regular intervals each day.

Rule Five: Exercise Every Day

We've said everything there is to say about exercise, with the single exception of the extraordinary role it plays in weight control. Not only does it remove pounds of body weight, it keeps them from returning—*something diet alone can never do.*

Exercise converts fat tissue into muscle. The more muscle gained, the greater the loss of body fat. Since muscle tissue weighs more than fatty tissue, the immediate consequence of exercise is a small increase in scale weight. But the mirror tells the important story: you look slimmer almost at once. The more exercise you do, the more calories you burn; the more you burn, the greater the decrease in fatty deposits. Eventually your overall weight drops as well.

Why does exercise produce a weight loss? The answer lies in what happens to the body's metabolic rate—the rate at which we burn or utilize calories to create energy.

We burn calories day and night, even when we're sleeping. Breathing, circulating the blood, turning in bed—all require energy. From the moment we awaken and get out of bed, our basal metabolic rate (BMR) rises in proportion to the intensity of activity. Early morning people who are roaring to go on arising raise their BMR earlier, and keep it higher longer, than do people who need several hours to get going. The BMR is highest during a workout or heavy labor—and that effort redounds to your benefit for hours after it has ended. Tests have shown that athletes maintain a 20 to 25 percent increase in their resting metabolic rate for twenty-four hours following a strenuous workout, burning more calories and storing less fat than normal. A reasonable workout does the same thing to a lesser degree.

Most BMRs decrease in late afternoon and early evening, an unfortunate circumstance given the predisposition of most people to eat their heaviest meal at dinner time despite all recommendations to the contrary. Excessive amounts of food eaten at a time of diminished activity obviously predispose us to store fat rather than burn calories.

How can we intervene in this unfortunate circumstance? By exercising just before dinner, even if it's nothing more than a brisk walk. That activity alone elevates our BMR. More important still, it fools our appetite center, a portion of our nervous system that dictates how hungry we are.

This appetite center is in the base of the brain, in a region known as the limbic area of the hypothalmus. It responds to chemicals carried to it by the blood. Exercise, even a brief, rapid walk, causes fat to be released from the fat cells and sugar to be released from the liver to supply energy for the exercise. The brain does not know that this food is coming from storage rather than from new supplies. It only knows that it's being appeased. Thus is the brain's hunger center fooled, and our appetite satisfied with less food when we begin to eat.

A brief walk after meals is an excellent idea as well; the body burns calories, thereby burning rather than storing some of the fats just consumed. If exercising on a full stomach makes you uncomfortable, wait fifteen to thirty minutes after your meal.

Exercise enhances weight loss in two additional ways. First, it raises body temperature; even a small increase in body temperature causes the body to burn more calories. Second, exercise burns fat and fat breaks down into ketones, acid substances that, when in the bloodstream, decrease the appetite.

In a variety of ways, therefore, exercise not only improves cardiovascular fitness but contributes to weight loss as well.

Notes of Caution: Good Habits in Bed with Bad

All your efforts will come to naught if you neutralize good habits with bad.

Do you smoke? Aside from ruining your cardiovascular system and raising the odds of lung cancer, you're impairing your digestion and destroying the vitamin C in your system.

Do you drink? There is absolutely nothing wrong with a glass or two of wine or beer with dinner. But anything more than that could be placing you beyond a safe drinking threshold, not only making you more vulnerable to physical problems but producing vitamin and mineral deficiencies.

If you drink wine or beer with meals, you should bear in mind that they are negative factors in weight control. Not only are they high in calories, they influence our sense of satiety, giving us the feeling that we need to eat more even though we may have already eaten enough.

Do you drink caffeinated beverages either before or during a meal? Coffee and tea, which have chemically irritating substances that decrease the efficiency of the digestive juices—exactly the opposite of wine and beer—decrease the benefits your body receives from the food you consume. So do soft drinks, antacids, and antibiotics.

Finally, a note about drinking water. Most people don't drink nearly enough, not during a normal working day, and not when they exercise.

The body needs great quantities of water to maintain its fluid balance and to keep the plumbing working. Drinking water *while* exercising—not just afterward—is extremely important. Exercise raises the body temperature, and water puts out the fire. Exercise increases the filtration of blood by the kidneys, draining fluid out in the process. It must be replaced. Exercise creates waste products that irritate the muscles; water washes these irritants out.

Whether you follow only one rule or a few rules or all five, you will quickly discover that they are mutually reinforcing. Just as with exercise, your body will quickly respond to the attention it's being paid. Looking better and feeling better, you'll find yourself highly motivated to stick to the Rejuvenating Menu.

14. AVOIDING ILLNESS

Supposing your doctor wrote out a prescription following your latest checkup and, handing it to you, said, "Here's a medication I want you to take. It will greatly lessen your chances of contracting half a dozen diseases you become increasingly vulnerable to after the age of thirty-five." Would you get the prescription filled and then take the medicine? Assuming there were no adverse side effects, the answer, in all probability, is "yes."

There is no one medication that can perform such a miracle, but there is a prescription nonetheless. The prescription is for an exercise—and maintenance—program precisely like the one we've set forth.

No doctor can compel a patient to take the medicine he or she has prescribed, and the sad reality is that some patients don't even bother to get their prescriptions filled. The reason for such self-destructive behavior varies with individuals, but one central explanation may be an unconscious belief that nothing can really help them. Some people may simply conclude that the ravages of aging are unavoidable and beyond our control.

I don't want you to believe that for a moment.

There are *at least* half a dozen diseases that can be fended off or avoided altogether with the help of an appropriate exercise program. There are no absolute guarantees, just as there are none where medications are concerned, but the evidence overwhelmingly suggests that you'd be well advised to follow the prescription.

Let's describe these diseases one by one, and demonstrate the role of exercise in prevention and cure.

Avoiding Degenerative Arthritis

This will sound familiar, but we'll review it once more because it's such a common crippler of persons past thirty-five.

Degenerative arthritis is an impairment of the joints that develops as we age. A small amount of arthritis is probably unavoidable, but most of it is a consequence of the splits, cracks, and fractures of cartilage caused by abuse or inactivity.

To avoid degenerative arthritis, we must avoid doing violence to the cartilage in our joints. That means that once we reach thirty-five we have to minimize traumatic exercises in favor of nontraumatic and non-weight-bearing ones. At the other end of the scale, we have to minimize neglect—by care, concern, and concrete action.

That's where exercise comes in.

We maintain the normal nutrition of joints by putting them through their full range of motion repeatedly during the day. To be kept from deteriorating, every joint has to be moved regularly and every muscle moving the joints has to be contracted. This movement and contraction will lubricate the joint, using fluids secreted from the cartilage by the pressure, just like water squeezed from a sponge. The same action will nourish the cartilage and eliminate its wastes.

In addition to warding off degenerative arthritis, proper exercise protects you against tendonitis. Tendons, those bands of dense, tough, inelastic, white, fibrous tissue that connect muscles to bones, have no significant blood supply of their own. They are rejuvenated by being stretched and put under tension. Exercise keeps them strong and lubricated.

Dealing with Diabetes

Diabetes, a disease that impairs the body's ability to use sugar and produces an abnormal amount of urine, occurs in older people much more frequently than in younger ones. Acquired diabetes results from the failure of the pancreas, a gland situated near the stomach, to secrete a sufficient amount of the hormone insulin, which helps the body burn off sugar. If diabetes isn't properly treated, it can result in premature death. For years, the traditional treatment has been artificial supplies of insulin. We now know that diabetes can be controlled, as well, by proper diet —and exercise.

A proper diet, especially for an elderly diabetic, is one that is high in protein and low in calories and fats. It's extremely important for the diabetic to keep his or her weight down, because the more fatty tissue there is, the greater the amount of insulin required to service it.

Exercise is important in two critical ways. First, it decreases the amount of fatty tissue. Second, it induces the body to produce every bit of insulin it can, and to use what insulin there is in the most efficient manner. Several topflight tennis players are severe diabetics. While they're competing, their need for artificial supplies of insulin is either eliminated or markedly decreased.

Assisting the Circulatory System

Arteriosclerosis is a disease of the arteries characterized by the inelasticity and thickening of the vessel walls. The consequence: lessened blood flow.

Atherosclerosis is a form of arteriosclerosis characterized by the deposit of fatty substances on the innermost lining of the arteries. The result is the same: lessened blood flow. Both forms of the disease tend to be found much more commonly in older rather than younger people.

Atherosclerosis, in particular, can be controlled by diet and exercise. It's extremely important to monitor cholesterol and triglyceride levels by having blood samples analyzed every year. Because we secrete our own cholesterol, we have to be careful about the amount of cholesterol we ingest.

In recent years, research scientists have discovered that exercise produces extra quantities of high-density lipoproteins, the so-called "good cholesterol," which function as scavengers in the arterial system, carrying off fatty deposits. The only other activity that is known to produce high-density lipoproteins is the ingestion of alcoholic beverages. There are no unpleasant side effects to sensible exercise; there almost always are in the consumption of more than two alcoholic drinks a day.

There are two other diseases of the circulatory system that benefit greatly from exercise. The first is hypertension, the medical term for high blood pressure. The *immediate* effect of exercise is to raise the blood pressure. The *long-term effect* is to lower it permanently. For anyone with hypertension, the prescription would seem to be daily doses of the kind of exercise that doesn't raise blood pressure precipitously but benefits the circulatory system over the long run.

The other circulatory disease beneficially affected by exercise is *claudication*, which is characterized by a deficient blood supply to the lower extremities. The problem originates in the blood vessels that supply blood to the leg muscles. When these vessels are impaired, the muscles can't get the blood they need. The result is pain and cramps, particularly when walking.

There are two remedies for this condition. The first is to eliminate even the simplest movements of the lower extremities. The second is to increase the amount of exercise, which will eventually create auxiliary blood vessels and send more adequate supplies of blood and oxygen to the limbs. It's as though you had a sprinkler system that couldn't adequately service your lawn. Your options would be to exclude certain parts of the lawn in order to water other parts well, or to build up the sprinkler system. Whether it's blood or water, the choice is pretty obvious.

No one knows exactly how the body produces supplementary blood vessels. All we really know is that activity stimulates the cells of the blood vessels to create new blood vessels. It's a function of supply and demand. Muscles need blood supplies in order to function; the blood supply, in turn, is totally dependent on the size and number of the blood vessels. When the blood supply is deficient—when exercise produces a demand for blood that isn't being met by the current delivery system—nature adds to the system, increasing both the number and the size of the vessels.

Checking Osteoporosis

Osteoporosis is a predominantly female condition, occurring any time from the age of forty-five to seventy. As a woman ages, hormonal changes along with changes in diet and activity cause a loss of calcium from the bones that is not replaced. The result is a diminished skeleton and bones so fragile that everyday actions such as stepping off a curb can result in a broken bone.

The diet of the menopausal or postmenopausal woman needs to include enough calcium not only to meet ordinary skeletal needs but to compensate for calcium loss in aging bones. But diet alone is neither the cause of osteoporosis nor its exclusive remedy. It doesn't do a blessed bit of good to consume a lot of calcium if that calcium doesn't get absorbed into the bones.

Absorption requires chemical help. Hormones provide that help in the mature woman, extracting calcium from the diet and bloodstream and depositing it into the bones. It's when production of the hormones decreases, as it does with the cessation of menstruation, that a woman becomes increasingly vulnerable to osteoporosis. For a long while the use of hormonal supplements was clouded by an increased risk of cancer. Today, that risk appears to have been sizably diminished by a combination of estrogen and progesterone that provide, in tandem, the benefits associated with hormone production. But the risk hasn't been eliminated altogether, the system is still not perfect, and tough choices still have to be made. Not even doctors are in agreement as to what course to take.

A second course of chemical help can come from the replacement of a lactate enzyme that is present during infancy but gradually disappears. The same enzyme, which helps the body absorb the calcium it ingests, is present in yogurt. One nutrition authority, Dr. Sam Bessman of the University of Southern California, has suggested that five pints of yogurt a week would prevent osteoporosis. (That amount of yogurt, alas, contains a frightful number of calories, which could produce a weight problem unless calories were diminished elsewhere in the diet.)

Milk, cheese, and other dairy products high in calcium are important dietary supplements for postmenopausal women. With these products, unwanted calories and cholesterol can often be avoided by using low-fat or nonfat products.

But diet, hormones and enzymes will not solve the problem alone. If you want to be certain to avoid osteoporosis, you have to exercise as well.

Research animals with adequate hormone production, adequate enzymes, and adequate amounts of calcium in their diets still lost calcium from their bones when they were kept from exercising. When they were made to move, calcium loss did not occur. To be deposited in the bone, calcium has to be brought to it; the most vigorous, vital means of that transportation is exercise.

Physical activity for a woman who wants to keep her bones strong and healthy must include gravity and weight-bearing exercise and muscle contraction. Walking rapidly, swimming, and bicycle riding will do the job. Strenuous house or lawn work can do it, too, provided it's truly strenuous, not just work. Unfortunately, household and garden chores are usually less than vigorous, however tiring—and certainly less fun than the other options.

Combating Depression

Depression is a companion of aging, as debilitating as any disease. It increases the velocity of aging, which makes the process, in turn, even less acceptable than it normally would be.

Numerically, depression is a significant disease. Among older people who visit doctors today, in addition to the physical complaint that takes them there, some 50 percent are suffering from some degree of depression.

The causes of depression are multiple. Some are clearly psychosocial. Men often become depressed as retirement nears or once it's a fact; they can't handle what they interpret as a loss of involvement and importance. In a society that emphasizes the virtues of youth as much as ours does, late middle-aged and elderly persons find themselves devalued and shunted to the side.

For a long while depression was treated almost exclusively with psychotherapy. Today we know that depression can also result from chemical imbalances, and there are drugs to correct such imbalances.

And then there is exercise, the most natural cure for depression, not simply because of its psychological reaffirmation of physical capacity but because of its chemical benefits as well.

As we've mentioned in several connections, exercise stimulates the production of endorphins, an antidepressant chemical created by the body in the limbic system of the hypothalmus. Those "highs" reported by runners are real, and any stimulating exercise—rapid walking, bicycling, skiing, swimming—can produce them.

So exercise can ward off degenerative arthritis, produce insulin naturally to deal with diabetes, help purge the arterial system of fatty deposits, lower blood pressure, create auxiliary blood vessels, combat osteoporosis, and cure or diminish depression. What drug could do all that?

15. STAYING YOUNG

Since 1900, average life expectancy has increased twenty-seven years—more in less than a century than the gain in the preceding five thousand years. Today, statistically at least, you can expect to live to age seventy-four; if you are still alive at the end of the century, your expectations should be even greater. Given the prospect of such a long life, would you not choose, if you could, to look and feel younger than you are in your later years, and be able to act younger as well? To *be*, in fact, younger than your years?

The option exists. It is yours for the taking. This isn't wishful, and it isn't conjecture. It is the central fact of aging. Let me state it once again: In later years, the biological variable in the human body can be as great as thirty years. At age sixty, you can have the body and appearance and stamina of a person forty-five—or seventy-five. It's entirely up to you.

Remember the sponge. Unused, it dries, shrinks, and cracks. This is exactly what happens to your body when it isn't used appropriately. But use it well and it springs to life again, giving you years of extra service.

Using your body well means not abusing it with violent exercise under the misguided notion that if it doesn't hurt, it isn't helpful. When it hurts, that's a certain sign that you've damaged your body. After thirty-five, recovery is never complete; there's always some residual damage.

But each day that you're *not* physically active is leaving its scars as well.

The prescription for youthfulness is time-tested. It works without question. There are no unpleasant side effects—provided you follow the prescription.

But note well: Your prescription is not the same as the next person's. It is relative to your age and your present physical condition. You are the best possible judge of what quantity of physical activity is right for you. No doctor in the world can tell you how you feel. It's important for you to check in with your doctor before embarking on an exercise program, particularly if there's been any personal or family history or sign of heart disease. But if you are a normally healthy person, and if you have a normal amount of common sense, you can moderate your own exercise program along the guidelines I've presented.

As your fitness level improves, your exertions can increase. Remember, too, that even as you increase the challenge, your perceived exertion will remain the same because you'll be in better shape.

And what an extraordinary feeling that is—to find yourself far more supple than you were a month before, to be able to walk for an hour at a vigorous clip where you once dragged through twenty minutes; to suddenly catch sight of yourself in a mirror or store window and realize that you look taller than you did only months before.

And look younger, as well.

"Look younger." What, truly, does that mean? What makes some sixty-year-olds look like forty-five and others like seventy-five? Two factors predominate. The first is our bearing. The second is our face. Of the first, a great deal has been said. Let us speak now of the second.

Maintaining a Youthful Face

What of the muscles of the face? Can anything be done to perpetuate their youth and vitality? Is exercise of value for these muscles as it is for the other muscles of the body? In a word, the answer is "yes."

The face mostly shows aging by changes of the skin, which thins and wrinkles. To a certain extent, these changes are inescapable. Wrinkling, in particular, is often hereditary and—like our ancestors—beyond our control.

But certain influences on the skin are controllable. Diet is one of them; a good balanced diet benefits the texture of the skin. Sunlight is another; we all love a tan, but too much exposure to the sun will produce premature wrinkles. Weight is a third influence; too much weight loss in too short a period also increases wrinkling, especially in the case of a heavy person whose underlying fat has overstretched the skin. *Gradual* weight loss is as important to cosmetics as it is to health.

Now, what of the facial muscles? Grouped around the mouth, eyes, and nose, they are all "sphincter" muscles, in that when they shorten, they narrow the opening of these orifices. The muscles of the face shorten permanently if they remain contracted for a long enough period of time, just as any muscles do. Keep your knees bent in a sitting position throughout each day without taking time to stretch them and you'll develop "adaptive shortening." Frown for a long enough period of time and it will actually hurt you to smile.

Like the other muscles in your body, the muscles of the face need to be exercised if they are to remain youthful. The following exercises are extremely simple, and should be done in front of a mirror.

Exercise 1. Shut your eyes, purse your lips, and squeeze the muscles of your nose as tightly as you can, until your face is as wrinkled as a prune. Hold the expression for five seconds.

Open wide, stretching your lips and eyes and flaring your nostrils. Hold that expression for five seconds.

Relax completely for five seconds.

Repeat the cycle five times.

Exercise 2. Place your index fingers half an inch from the outer corners of your eyes, and pull gently until the eyes are narrow slits. Hold for five seconds.

With the fingers still in place, try to draw the outer corners of the eyes in toward your nose. Hold for five seconds.

Repeat the cycle five times.

Exercise 3. Place your index fingers half an inch from the corners of your mouth, and pull gently until the lips will stretch no farther. Hold for five seconds.

With the fingers still in place, try to purse your lips as tightly as you can. Hold for five seconds.

Repeat the cycle five times.

But more than exercise is involved in the maintenance of a youthful face.

Like the other muscles of the body, the facial muscles are under voluntary control, but—again like the other muscles—they respond to the emotions, which often aren't under voluntary control.

Facial muscles are muscles of expression. "You look happy . . . sad . . . tense . . . uptight . . . depressed . . . tired." You can read these emotions in body language. You can read them even more readily in the face. Tension tightens the facial muscles. Anger contorts them. Depression makes them droop.

No facial exercises can fully counteract the damage to the muscles of the face of a lifetime of feeling uptight. To avoid such damage, prevent further damage, or repair the existing damage to any degree at all, you have to deal with the emotions.

The causes of emotional problems may well be deep-seated and require professional care. But psychiatrists wouldn't argue with the proposition that fitness is an important component of psychological wellness. "People who are productive stay healthy, and if you remain healthy you're more apt to be productive," Dr. Robert Butler, formerly head of the National Institute on Aging, has said. Let me paraphrase and adapt that just a bit: People who are fit tend to be more optimistic, and if you remain optimistic, you're more apt to remain fit—and look it.

You *Are* as Young as You Feel

Exercise elevates the mood by increasing stores of energy and simultaneously secreting adrenalin-like substances in the body that act as stimulants and antidepressants. That increased feeling of well-being transmits itself to the body. The taut muscles of the face relax. The sagging body straightens.

The way we look and carry ourselves is not simply a physical matter. It is an expression of how we feel about ourselves, and about life in general. What keeps people going is the prospect that tomorrow will be more rewarding than today. That thought alone will remove the lines from your face and set your body straight—provided, of course, that you believe tomorrow *will* be more rewarding.

Knowing that you're in shape to deal with tomorrow is an important component of such a belief. Being in shape is a mental as well as a physical process. The mind is like a muscle in one respect: It deteriorates if it isn't used. It's confidence and enthusiasm that persuade us to engage our minds as well as our bodies. That kind of mood is bound up, in turn, in how we feel about ourselves physically.

There is no direct relationship between being physically active and retaining a sharp mind, but there is a very definite correlation. To maintain an agile mind, you have to be out in the world, where the brain has a chance to be stimulated. To transport yourself to and through this world, you need a fit body.

People who are alone age much faster than those who share their lives with others. People alone spend most of their time sitting, don't communicate, and become more and more reclusive. They stop talking and reading, and eventually stop thinking. Their minds deteriorate just like their bodies.

To keep your body going, you should never stop exercising. To keep your mind going, you should never retire. When your career ends, find a second and even a third one. Become a partisan of a political cause, a charity, even a team—something that will rouse your passions, get you involved, and keep you moving.

In one sense, youthfulness can be defined as an absence of pain, discomfort, or disability—from either mental or physical causes. We age to the extent that we acquire those liabilities. We remain young to the extent that we avoid them.

We can't avoid aging any more than we can avoid death. What we *can* do is delay and even reverse the effects of aging, making ourselves as youthful as possible for as long as possible.

What a splendid option. As we young folks say, *"Go for it."*

ACKNOWLEDGMENTS

We are grateful to all those at Doubleday & Company who took such special care with this book, and especially grateful for their advice and attention to Sam Vaughan, Doubleday's former editor in chief, and to our indefatigable editor, Jim Moser.

Deborah Davies, who did the illustrations, performed beautifully under intense deadline pressure.

Jacquelyn Gross contributed important editorial help in the early stages, and she and Lois Cailliet were critical readers of each draft.

Finally, we would like to thank our agent, Sterling Lord, for finding the right home for this book.

RENÉ CAILLIET
LEONARD GROSS